APPRECIATION

I would like to express my sincere appreciation to Mark Hooker, my longtime friend, for listening to my book idea five years ago and encouraging me. I would also like to thank Mark for his feedback on some of the writing in the early stages and for his comments on the illustrations. I would also like to thank Lorrie Kazan and Susan Hartman for their thoughts. Thanks to longtime friends Clive Edwards and Scott Swaney, and also to my friend Luise Foertsch, for their positive outlook and belief in me. And thank you, thank you, thank you, Bruce Kaye, another longtime good friend, for your help with everything.

I would also like to express deep gratitude to four individuals who supported me on my spiritual path the past five years as I went through many inner changes: Connie Bender, Karen Mills-Alston, Maggie Erickson, and Valerie Wolf. You all know the part you played. Thank you.

Finally, I would like to express appreciation to my parents, Louis and Phyllis. Both passed away quickly, earlier this year (2013), my father shortly after my mother, just after their 65th wedding anniversary. Dad, it meant so much to me last year when you told me how much you loved Mom. You stayed by her, and then followed her. I miss you both very much.

Face Reading for Love

Understand yourself, your partner,
your date, or your lover!

DEBRA JEANE HOULE, L.Ac., M.A.T.C.M.

© 2013 Debra Jeane Houle
All Rights Reserved.

No part of this publication may be reproduced, stored in a retrieval system, or transmitted, in any form or by any means, electronic, mechanical, photocopying, recording, or otherwise, without the written permission of the author.

First published by Dog Ear Publishing
4010 W. 86th Street, Ste H
Indianapolis, IN 46268
www.dogearpublishing.net

dog ear
PUBLISHING

ISBN: 978-1-4575-2361-8

This book is printed on acid-free paper.

Printed in the United States of America

Author photograph by Anthony Evergreen

TABLE OF CONTENTS

SECTION I – THE BASICS: Begin Face Reading

INTRODUCTION...2

We express in our unique way 2
A brief history of Face Reading 2
Face reading for love 3

SUGGESTIONS FOR USING THIS BOOK..........5

Jumping around is perfectly okay 5
Begin with yourself 5
Learn about your partner 6
Learn about your date - or learn how to find a mate 7
Learn about others 8

GIFTS AND CHALLENGES 9

HOW TO READ A FACE...11

PRIORITY REGIONS...13

Measure physically or visually 13
The Priority Region reveals a person's priority 14

THE TWO SIDES 20

BROAD AND NARROW 22

The wider the face, the more outgoing and confident 22

BASIC FACE SHAPES 25

The basic shape reveals the basic character 25

SECTION II –
THE DETAILS: Reading Features

THE FEATURES 32

THE EARS 33

High ears reveal high speed; low reveals slow 33
Ears that stick out reveal a desire to stand out 35
Size suggests listening ability and how hearing is handled 39
The shape of the ear affects what one hears 42
Slant suggests outlook 46
Width reveals risk-taking 47
Earlobes show stability and appreciation for the material world 52
Lobe attachment tells of a desire to remain attached 56
Circles reveal inner or outer listening 59
The feeling of the firmness reveals the firmness of the feelings 60
Very red suggests the heart rules the head 61
Lost hair from the head might be found in the ears 62

THE HAIRLINE 64

Shape shows interest in ideas, others, or business 64
Hairlines wide don't hide 67
Low hairlines last longer 69
A rough edge suggests a rough beginning 70

THE FOREHEAD 72

The top tells of inherited talents 72
Learning style is learned from the slant; creativity is seen
    in the curve 73
Span of interests is shown in the width 76
Short suggests a down-to-earth focus 78

THE EYEBROWS 81

Approach to life and thinking shows in the shape 81
Slant projects presence 85
Passion is revealed in the thickness 86
Time to act is told in the distance 89
Space suggests span of interests 91
Length leads to friendships 94
Distribution determines the gift 95
Orderly brows, orderly thoughts 100
Feel the feel for feelings 101

THE EYEBROW RIDGE 103

A defined ridge shows a desire to be the authority 103

THE EYELIDS 105

Connection can be found in no fold 105
Eyelids expose intimacy requirements 106
Puffs indicate a need to let go 109
The eyes are open, but are you being let in? 111

THE EYES 114

Eye size shows the size of the heart's opening 114
For point of view, look where the eyes point 117
Space shows span of focus 119
Depth discloses eagerness to relate 121
The eyes' shapes tell time spent thinking 123
Color communicates too! 127
Movement throws others off balance 132

THE TEMPLES 133

A temple might be a holy place 133

THE NOSE 135

Size suggests the need to make a statement 135
Length reveals planning time needed 138
A protruding nose shows a pioneering personality 139
Work style is shown in the shape 141
Energy for work is found across the bridge 143
A high level of self-will is seen in a High Bridge 146
Bumps reveal a spirited individual 147
Desire to save may be seen in the tip 149
The nose tip direction points out one's point of view 151
The bigger the holes, the more money flows 153
Nose wings show protection and support 156

THE PHILTRUM and the UPPER LIP 158

The groove gives clues to how one might want to be seen 158
A long space suggests high self-esteem 159

THE MOUTH 161

The width of the mouth whispers or shouts 161
For expectations of things turning out, look at the turn
    of the mouth 164

THE LIPS 166

Expressiveness is found in the fullness 166
The two lips represent the two worlds 169
Bottoms are bigger 171
When lips stick out, thoughts are spoken out 172

THE TEETH 175

When talking of teeth, size and shape matter 175

THE CHIN 179

A strong chin reveals a strong will 179
Style of action is shown in the shape 181
Stubbornness can be seen from the side 184

THE JAW 187

Strength is seen in the width 187

THE CHEEKS and the CHEEKBONES 189

Noticeable bones get noticed 189
Life can be seen in the fullness 192

SECTION III- ANOTHER LOOK:
The Face and the Five Chinese Elements

WOOD 196

Expanding their mind is more important than expanding their wallet 199

FIRE 201

Fire gets noticed and Fire Individuals want to be 202
Fire likes what looks hot but is adverse to heat 203

EARTH 205

Earth is stable but might fall into a rut 206

METAL 208

Metal itself is hard, and Metal Individuals are hard on themselves 209

WATER 211

Water might lounge in the tub but may swim in money 212

LOVE IS AN ACTIVITY OF CONSCIOUSNESS 215

BIBLIOGRAPHY 217

CONTACT INFORMATION 219

PREFACE

Face Reading is an ancient art with roots in Chinese Medicine. Although I had read some on the subject many years earlier, I officially began my study of Face Reading in 1997 while working towards my Master's degree at Yo San University of Traditional Chinese Medicine in Los Angeles. Because I wanted to learn all that I could, I enrolled in many non-required classes. I took a class on Chinese Face Reading. My instructor was Lillian Bridges, an internationally acclaimed speaker and teacher on the subject. Later, a few years into my acupuncture practice, I looked over my class notes and they re-sparked my interest in Face Reading.

This book is my interpretation of the subject of Face Reading that has emerged from extensive research, general observations, interactions with friends, professional client readings, and insights I received during daily life and meditation.

My intent for this book is that it awakens readers to their talents, strengths, challenges, and gifts as revealed in their face. My desire also is that this book leads to greater understanding of others, and more harmonious relationships. My dream is that it brings more acceptance, compassion, and LOVE to the world.

I created the drawings, which are basic and to the point. I loved writing and illustrating this book. I hope you find it informative, helpful, and enjoyable.

Section I

THE BASICS:

Begin Face Reading

INTRODUCTION

There are no "good" or "bad" faces and no face is "ideal"
But, a face tells of gifts and challenges
And much more a face can reveal

We express in our unique way

What reveals how quickly a person wants to get close? What tells of work style and money? What elemental type talks with their hands? What suggests an addictive personality? The answers are in this book.

We are all individuals who express in *our* unique way. As individuals we see things *our* way, hear things *our* way, speak things *our* way, and do things *our* way. We interpret life *our* way, which we often feel is the right way. However, we don't always understand *our* way, and we understand others even less.

Gain a better understanding of yourself using the ancient art of face reading. If you are in a relationship with a partner you wish to know more about, or if you are looking for a partner just right for you, read this book, as it can help with that too!

A brief history of Face Reading

The systematic art of face reading originated in ancient China over 2,500 years ago. Faces were originally read by Chinese medical doctors for the purpose of diagnosing health. Physicians subsequently found that an individual's character, gifts, strengths, and talents were revealed in the face.

Face reading became a respected art practiced by well-educated men who advised and counseled their clients. The practice was popular throughout China, spread to Japan and India, and found its way to the Greek and Egyptian cultures. Hippocrates wrote about face reading, and Aristotle is credited with the first systematic treatise on the subject.

Face reading reached Europe in the late 1200s and became known as physiognomy. In 1272 Michael Scott, a highly educated man who received one of the most expensive educations of that time, wrote *Physiognomia Et De Hominis Proceatione*. It was published in eighteen editions. Physiognomy was well accepted and taught in universities. Unfortunately, it fell into disrespect years later when practiced by less than respectable individuals such as vagabonds and swindlers.

In the late 18th century, face reading enjoyed a strong revival due to Swiss theologian and scientific writer Johann Kaspar Lavater. He wrote *Essays on Physiognomy*. His writings drew international attention and he became well known throughout Europe.

The popularity of face reading grew and circled the globe. The connection between an individual's inner nature and its outward manifestation appeared in the works of many well-known novelists. Even former United States President Abraham Lincoln found face reading useful. It is said he used it to help select his cabinet.

In 1913 *The Encyclopedia of Face and Form Reading* was written by Mary Olmstead Stanton and published in Philadelphia. It contains 1203 pages, small print, and long outdated words not easily understood. This and the fact that it reflects some of the prejudices prevailing during that time period make reading it difficult. However, the book also includes nearly four hundred exceptionally detailed illustrations. Well received when released one century ago, it is a major contribution to the subject of Face Reading.

In the last century, more has been learned and more books have been written. Ancient wisdom has been updated to fit with modern times. Interest in the subject is currently growing.

Face reading for love

Read this book for a better understanding of yourself. Learn why you hear, think, see, speak, and act the way that you do. Discover your gifts, strengths, and challenges, too. To love yourself, you need to be you. Doing what others do may not be the right fit. Gain a greater appreciation for who you are!

Face Reading for Love can help you find new things to love about your partner. Understanding can replace misunderstandings and critical judgment. This book was written to enlighten, with examples often presented in a lighthearted way. With greater awareness, you may lighten up as well.

Keep in mind when reading your face, or that of another, that the information revealed tells of tendencies and not absolutes.

If you are seeking a relationship, this book can be beneficial. *Face Reading for Love* can help you understand your date or may help in finding a partner. The essence of one's being is revealed in the face, so look to the face to see what it has to say. And, you might want to know what you are looking for when looking at a face. If you're seeking an intellectual person, for example, you may be interested to learn that those with a mental focus tend to have a large forehead. If you're looking for a person who fights for what he or she believes, look for a prominent jaw and a strong, broad chin. This powerful combination suggests strong sexual potential, which may also be important to you.

As you express kindness, understanding, and sincerity to others, you attract kind, understanding, and sincere individuals into your life.

Face Reading for Love is useful for understanding friends, family, dates, and workmates. There are many types of relationships and unlimited opportunities to love. We are all different, and yet we are all equal. Although we express ourselves as individuals, in truth we are one.

SUGGESTIONS FOR USING THIS BOOK

Jumping around is perfectly okay

There is no right or wrong way to use this book. You might enjoy reading it from beginning to end. But if you see a face or feature you are curious about, you might want to look among these pages to see what it reveals. How you use this book is up to you, but for those who would like some suggestions, here are a few.

Begin with yourself

1. Although this book was written using words to help you understand others, you can also use it to understand yourself. Read with a mirror at hand, and start with the basics. Read the introductory chapters (Section I) and begin to see what your face reveals.

2. Then, read about the facial features (Section II) with a focus on details. Features that stand out provide the strongest clues to one's character. Start with your features that you notice first or features about which you are most aware.

3. Next, look at features about which you wish to know more, even if these features aren't ones that (on you) stand out. For example, you may wish to know what a chin can reveal.

   When reading a face it is important to remember that an individual's character is not made up of just one or two features. Although the most notable features provide the strongest clues to character, a person's personality is revealed by the face shape and the combination of all the features. It is important not to assess your character, or that of another, based on features viewed in isolation.

4. To learn about your face from a different point of view, read Section III: The Face and the Five Chinese Elements. Discover your elemental type and find out how you energetically express in the world.

5. Finally, when learning about yourself, you might want to look at your face for clues about your perfect job or career. Your face can help reveal the type of work for which you have a talent or gift. You may already have a feeling about this work; it is likely something you long to do. Your face might confirm that it is what you are meant to do, giving you courage to do it. And, if you are already doing this work, your face can confirm you are on the right track.

Learn about your partner

An intimate relationship can offer emotional support and bring joy into an individual's life; it can assist personal growth and spiritual development. But being in a close relationship with another person is rarely easy.

Face reading can help you know your significant other better. A sincere desire to understand leads to better understanding. For more harmony in your relationship, when reading your partner's face, come from a place of love.

1. If you don't want your partner to know you are reading his or her face, don't stare, and check out only one thing at a time. Or, look at photos of your partner to do the face reading.

2. Review the basics (Section I) and begin learning what your partner's face reveals.

3. Next, look at the details (Section II). What are your partner's most noticeable features? Check them out. Then, look up other features about which you wish to know more.

4. To learn how your partner energetically expresses in the world, go to The Face and the Five Chinese Elements (Section III).

Reading your partner's face can bring greater awareness of how he or she might be experiencing life and may bring to light thought and emotional reaction patterns he or she is likely to have. You cannot change your partner, but you do have the ability to change how you think of and react to your partner. Face reading can give you knowledge of your partner's challenges and appreciation of his or her gifts.

Learn about your date— or learn how to find a mate

This book can be helpful when dating or seeking a relationship. The face gives clues to the nature within. The desire for intimacy is also revealed. See what the book says about eyes and eyelids to learn more about this.

If you have already read your own face, you are likely more aware of your nature, your gifts, and your talents. This knowledge can give you a stronger sense of self, which might make a strong impression on your date.

It is important to know who you are, what qualities you desire in another, what type of relationship you want, and what level of closeness is best for you. Know whether you even want a relationship! Some people just prefer friends or lovers. To find someone right for you, you need to be you; otherwise, you'll end up with someone best suited for someone else. Are you seeking passion and excitement or is security and stability most important to you?

Below are possible approaches to finding a date, lover, or partner. If you are currently dating someone, follow the steps in the previous section to better understand the individual you are seeing.

1. If seeking a date, lover, or partner, the basic nature of one's being is revealed in the face. You may thus find it helpful to *first read the book and then read the face*. When reading the book, if you come across a quality, ability, or personality trait you desire in another, note where it is revealed on the face.

2. You may be a person who feels strongly about features you find very attractive and have certain types to which you are physically attracted. Perhaps you find deep-set eyes extremely appealing. If so, look in the book to learn what they mean.

3. You may prefer having no image of what the person you are seeking should look like. If so, stay open and receptive as you go about your life, giving no thought to how things will come about or in what form your date, lover, or partner will manifest. Turn it over; trust, believe. After you have a connection with someone, read the face to gain a greater understanding of him or her.

Look at all individuals through eyes of understanding rather than judgment. Everyone is good at the core. Expressing love in what you think, say, and do, can bring someone wonderful to you!

Learn about others

Face reading can be valuable in understanding family, neighbors, workmates, and friends. Read faces to find out why certain people are the way they are.

Although you can never truly know what it is like to be another, a sincere desire to understand leads to greater understanding. No one is living life as you, and most do not believe as you do. Use this book to learn more about others. Remember that all individuals, in all situations, are doing the best they can.

Acknowledge your own shortcomings, and you may have an easier time accepting what you think of as undesirable character traits in others. Focus on positive qualities and that is more of what you will see.

GIFTS AND CHALLENGES

The face reveals gifts and challenges. Although this book does not always use the word "gifts" to describe personal qualities, gifts are an individual's *talents, strengths, abilities, and positive character traits* as revealed in the face. Gifts are provided for a purpose. Activating potential can bring bliss and joy to life! A successful life is one of service to others. Using one's gifts can help humanity as a whole.

Those who believe in reincarnation may say that before incarnating into an earth-bound body, an individual's soul identifies what life experiences it needs to grow. For those with this belief, these life experiences or life lessons are revealed in the face. Other individuals believe in only one lifetime on earth, believing that God made everyone with a Divine mission in mind. The face of these believers gives clues to their purpose. Some have no belief in God or in reincarnation, and many give no thought to their reason for being. But all are bestowed with talents, strengths, and gifts.

"Challenges" refers to difficulties that might be physical, mental, or emotional or difficulties due to some not-so-desirable aspects of one's personality. Awareness is the first step in transforming challenges.

Gifts can contain potential challenges. Close Set Eyes provide an example of this. In all of nature, function is determined by form. Close Set Eyes reveal gifts of enhanced concentration and the ability to see details and spot errors quickly. Close Set Eyes indicate an individual who has an easier time staying focused, which is helpful in achieving goals. But those with Close Set Eyes often have challenges seeing the big picture, may be narrow minded, and might focus too much on faults in others.

People can and do change and most often the face will reflect the change. But inner changes can be made while outer features stay the same. For example, a person with Close Set Eyes may have become aware of his or her narrow way of seeing things and is now more tolerant of other people and their viewpoints; yet, his or her eyes remain close together. Nevertheless, most often when a change is made on the inside, over time, the face will alter its appearance to reflect the change.

When an individual changes his or her way of thinking, acting, or being in the world in a positive way, one affirmative sign is likely to be seen. One's face will always appear more attractive from the inner glow, which comes from the heart.

A person's face does not decide his or her destiny. *What a person does with gifts, talents, challenges, and spiritual achievement decides his or her destiny.*

HOW TO READ A FACE

When you look at a face, what do you notice first? The features to which your eyes are first drawn provide the strongest clues to a person's nature. Features that appear *very* large, *very* small, *very* unusual, or *very* angular, straight, or curved are the features you may want to read first. When assessing size, compare the size of the feature with the size of the face.

The more extreme a face shape or feature, the more the information about it will apply. For example, information about a Narrow Face will apply more to an individual with a *very* Narrow Face than one with a face that is only *somewhat* narrow.

Many faces or features are moderate in shape or size. *Moderation indicates a blending of extremes and brings a gift for fitting in easily with others. The more moderation found in a face, the more likely this will be.* Moderate face shapes and features are not described in this book.

Although a face shape or feature may be moderate, you might find it very interesting to read about what various face shapes and features can reveal.

To read a face most accurately, the face needs to be at a straight angle and at your eye level. The chin should not be tilted up or down. This is especially important when reading the height of the ears.

Although the most noticeable features provide the strongest clues to an individual's nature, when reading a face, a person's character should not be assessed based on one or two features apart from the rest.

The right and left side of a face can be very different. Read the chapter, "The Two Sides," for more information on this phenomenon.

Informed face reading can be helpful in understanding yourself and others, but individuals are infinitely complex; a face reveals tendencies and not absolutes. And remember, an undesirable personality trait may have been overcome, but the potential challenge may still be revealed on the face.

Furthermore, although face reading is useful, it only goes so far. Each individual is unique and much more than that which can be read from a face or from words in a book.

PRIORITY REGIONS

Priority Regions, as termed in this book, are also known as the Three Zones or Three Regions. A Priority Region reveals how one relates to the world, makes known general focus, and tells how decisions are best made.

Measure physically or visually

Dividing a face into three horizontal regions, the longest is the Priority Region. Region 1 is the forehead; it runs from the original hairline to the top of the eyebrows. Region 2 is the middle of the face; it runs from the top of the eyebrows to the bottom of the nose. Region 3 begins at the bottom of the nose and ends at the bottom of the chin.

Regions can often be assessed visually; when a region is large or very long, this is easy to see. In many instances, facial features stand out and give clues to a person's Priority Region. For example, when a person has *high eyebrows and a very large nose* Region 2 is likely the longest region and thus the Priority Region.

You can also measure regions physically. You can use your hand as a measuring device. To do this, place your index finger on the top border of a region and your thumb on the bottom border. Measure all three regions in this manner to determine the longest. If the person doesn't know he or she is being read, you won't be able to use this measuring method.

And, if you have to physically measure, it may be too close to call. Some faces are equal in all three regions. When all three regions equal in length, there is no region of dominance and thus no Priority Region.

Many peoples have two Priority Regions. For example, a person might have a tall forehead, a long nose, and a short chin. Two equally long regions reveal areas of equal importance, and therefore two Priority Regions. In the example above, Region 3 is the shortest. Following explanations of Priority Regions are brief paragraphs on short regions for those who are interested.

The Priority Region reveals a person's priority

The Priority Region gives clues to what is important to an individual. Understanding Priority Regions can be valuable when dating and in romantic partnerships. Oftentimes opposites seem to attract. A person might pair with an individual with a different Priority Region in an attempt to balance what he or she feels is missing. But, understanding differences can sometimes be difficult for those who have dominance in different regions. Couples with facial regions in the same proportions tend to have an easier time relating to one another. The Priority Region reveals *area of focus*.

REGION 1 LONGEST – MENTAL PRIORITY

Region 1 runs from the hairline to the top of the eyebrows. If the individual is balding, imagine, if you can, where the hairline previously began. Those who are longest in Region 1 are Mental Priority Individuals. *Thinking is their focus*; they relate to the world through their mind and may have trouble getting out of their head.

Mental Priority Individuals are driven by ideas, need to be mentally stimulated, and may not see money as important as the opportunity to use their mental gift. Mental Priority Individuals often use long words, complicated sentences, abstract concepts, intellectual ideas, or technical terms in their day-to-day life. Some excel using logic and facts; others have creativity as their gift and use their mind in imaginative ways. Scientists, writers, composers, professors, and philosophers typically have tall foreheads and therefore Region 1 dominance.

It can make a Mental Priority Individual happy if people think he or she is smart.

Mental Priority Individuals need time to make decisions. They analyze situations and think things through. They need complete explanations and need details. Feelings might not play an important part; indeed, for those dominant in this region, their head rules their heart. A pro and con list might be useful when it comes to making decisions. Although most Mental Priority Individuals are slow decision makers, an individual with a forehead that sharply slants back suggests one who decides faster. If pushed for an answer, a Mental Priority Individual is likely to say "no."

If intellectual interests appeal to you, you will likely be attracted to a person with a Mental Priority.

A Mental Priority partner will tend to be energized challenging his or her mind, but may not have the same energy for physical pursuits. If physical activity is important to you, you might be working out by yourself. Perhaps give your thinking partner some thought out, researched, and proven data on the benefits of exercise to analyze.

A date with a very large Region 1 is a Mental Priority Individual. He or she might use big words with meanings that may be hidden from you. If your date is male, his private parts are also likely to be hidden, at least, at first. In case you were wondering, there is no place on the face that tells if these private parts might be big.

REGION 1 SHORTEST

When the forehead is the shortest region, it reveals that this individual is *least focused mentally or intellectually*. A short Region 1 suggests one who relates to the world in an emotional, material, or physical way. These individuals tend to be determined and persistent.

REGION 2 LONGEST – PRACTICAL PRIORITY

Region 2 runs from the top of the eyebrows to the bottom of the nose. Those longest in this area are Practical Priority Individuals. *Their focus is on practicality and ambition.*

Practical Priority Individuals relate to the world in a very human way; they desire to acquire, accomplish, and succeed. Many have an easier time finding their position in life, because to them finding it is a priority. Practical Priority Individuals tend to be logical and realistic. Most often they are very ambitious.

A large nose is often found when the center of a face dominates. The nose relates to work, power, and money, and a large nose show emphasis on these things. Being recognized for achievements is important to these individuals. Many seek quality, luxury, and status, and some seek a partner with money and status. Successful businesspeople often are Practical Priority Individuals.

Some Practical Priority Individuals seek to make the world a better place. They expand awareness outside of themselves and focus on global human needs.

Notably, some Practical Priority Individuals are not overly ambitious. With their practical priority, money is still very important, but their focus is on bargains and basic security. They have fundamental needs. These Practical Priority Individuals make decisions based on what is practical, useful, and logical.

It is important to Practical Priority Individuals not to waste time, energy, or money; they want value and results. Practical Priority Individuals, who choose to attend college, tend to major in a subject that leads to a career that provides stability or that pays well.

Challenges for Practical Priority Individuals can arise when too much importance is put on self, material things, or money; they may have challenges with those who waste time, energy, or money. Some Practical Priority Individuals have challenges spending money. Even if they are very rich, they may be very frugal.

If you have a Practical Priority partner, he or she may be very ambitious, both a challenge and a gift. Making money to save or spend may be put ahead of making time with you. Perhaps you are working hard too. Time off for holidays or weekends may lose out to money to be made. Vacations may be canceled if work calls. If money is very important to you as well, a hard-working Practical Priority partner may be an appreciated gift. Be sure to let him or her know he or she is appreciated.

If single and looking for a partner with real-world common sense, a Practical Priority partner might be a good choice.

REGION 2 SHORTEST

When the face is shortest in the middle, it reveals an individual who is not ego-based. These individuals can make lots money but *tend not to be materialistic*. The challenge for those with a short middle region is that they may not always be practical. Some work very hard for little recognition. It is not their focus to call attention to themselves. When working they get to the point and get the job done.

REGION 3 LONGEST – PHYSICAL PRIORITY

Region 3 extends from the bottom of the nose to the end of the chin. If the chin is double, only consider the first one. An individual with Region 3 longest is a Physical Priority Individual. These individuals *focus on the physical*; they enjoy things that are physical, and many are quite sexual as well. Physical Priority Individuals relate to the world through their physicality and "gut" instinct. When this part of the face is the longest, intuition plays a major role in the decisions these individuals make.

Physical Priority Individuals with a *strong jaw and chin* are often gifted athletes. Physical Priority Individuals who love cooking, comfort, and pleasures tend to show *roundness and softness* here. A long lower face tells of endurance. For Physical Priority Individuals, the best years may come later in life; many have a strong will to live and live a long time.

Physical Priority Individuals have the gift of a sharp intuition and can know something immediately without reasoning or being taught. They think best when doing something physical. Concentrated, focused thinking can confuse matters. Although Physical Priority Individuals make decisions quickly by nature, too many facts to analyze and consider adds stress, slows them down, and blocks easy access to their gift of intuition.

Physical Priority Individuals are gifted in performing work that is physical. They are good using their hands. With their restless nature, they find it challenging to be stuck day after day behind a desk. Other challenges can arise as well. Physical Priority Individuals sometimes respond quickly without giving thought to a matter or act without thinking things through. However, if guided by their powerful sixth sense, what they said or what they did was what they needed to have said or done.

Intuition is not based on logic or reason or practicality. If your partner is a Physical Priority Individual, the decisions he or she makes will not always make sense to you.

Although your Physical Priority partner might be quite aware of his or her feelings, he or she may have difficulty expressing them, especially when sitting still. You may find conversation flows easier when talking while walking.

If you are a Physical Priority Individual use your gift of intuition when dating. Trust your gut feelings. If a person doesn't *feel right* to you, he or she *isn't right* for you.

REGION 3 SHORTEST

When the bottom part of the face is shortest, it reveals *being physical is not a priority*. This individual will likely place higher priority on using his or her mind or making good use of his or her time or money. Intuitive thoughts may be disregarded or not acted upon. Thoughts of exercising may also be pushed aside.

A HIGHER PRIORITY

Individuals with the same Priority Regions typically have an easier time understanding each other; those with different Priority Regions often need to work harder to understand each other. For some however, the three regions are of less importance than they are for others. Those drawn together based on a spiritual connection find that individual differences are overcome. All phases of their relationship harmoniously fall into place. These individuals have a common meeting ground on which they unite. Living *a spiritually based life is their shared focus* and highest priority. When it comes to their faces, they may look similar or may look very different.

THE TWO SIDES

The two sides of a person's face correspond to the two sides a person's nature. The right is the public side; the business, linear, and logical side. The right side reveals what an individual shows to the world. The left half of the brain controls the right side of the body and face.

The left side of the face is the private side. The left side corresponds to inner thoughts and emotions. The left side of the body and face are controlled by the right half of the brain.

All faces become somewhat asymmetrical as people age; minor differences are not particularly important. Minor differences are often not noticed as the two sides of the face blend when viewing. However, if one side is *very different* than the other side, a person might look like two different people.

Sometimes, it is not the entire face, but only one feature that stands out as being different on the left and right. For example, the right eyebrow may be straight and the left eyebrow extremely curved.

Acting different in one's public and private life is sometimes necessary for high profile individuals and this can lead to the two sides looking unalike. Two very different sides may also be seen on those working in careers that don't express who they really are, or when a person is in a long term relationship that is not a match for his or her true self.

When both sides of a face are *very* different an individual might act like two different people. Big differences in the two sides of a face can reveal a person who goes back and forth on decisions and/or has mood swings. Balance is important in all aspects of life. One may have an easier life when both sides of the face are balanced.

If you are newly involved with a very asymmetrically faced individual, be aware of the potential for mood swings and/or wavering on decisions. It may take longer to get to know who this person is. If you have been involved with a very asymmetrically faced individual for some time, you are likely aware of the potential for changes in decisions, mood, and/or personality. If you have a very asymmetrical face, you may be aware of the very different sides of your nature and how this affects you and others.

BROAD AND NARROW

One of the first things you may notice about a face is its width. Some faces are very broad and some very narrow. The underlying bone structure gives a face its width.

The wider the face, the more outgoing and confident

Big bones form a sturdier face. Broader faces have bigger bones. Narrower faces have smaller bones and tend to be more delicate. Face width tells of *confidence and stamina*.

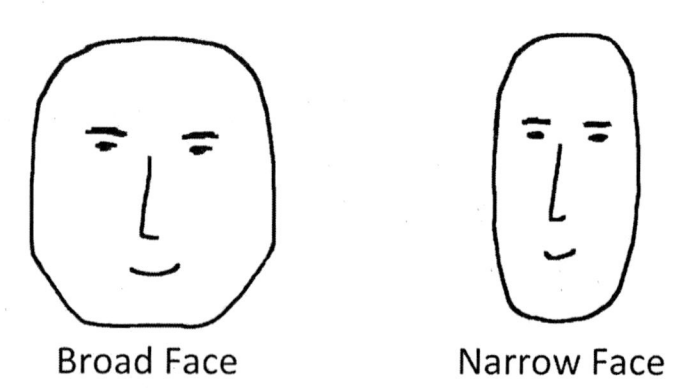

Broad Face   Narrow Face

BROAD FACE

A Broad Face reveals confidence and an outgoing individual with an abundance of stamina. Broad Face Individuals have the ability to deal with a wide variety of people and situations for a long time before becoming tired. They have a social nature and the energy for it.

A Broad Face suggests the gift of a strong belief in self. When these individuals desire to do something, they do it. It doesn't matter if they have not done it before; they feel no need to know everything first. But sometimes they take on too much or may not be prepared for what they take on.

Getting in over their head by taking on too much is more likely if a Broad Face is also a *short* face. A *short* Broad Face tells of extra fast action. These individuals get things done quickly, but can be impulsive, and a quick temper is a possible challenge. However, they tend to spend less time worrying.

Your Broad Face partner is likely to have confidence that spans a broad range. You know that your partner doesn't know everything. To keep the peace, there is no need to tell him, her, or anyone else. At times, your partner may speak with confidence when he or she tells you what you know is not true, or when he or she tells you what is just right for you. Listen and consider, but have confidence in yourself and what you know.

NARROW FACE

A Narrow Face reveals an independent nature and the gift of sensitivity. Narrow Face Individuals tend to have confidence restricted to a narrow range of topics. They have less stamina; their face suggests energy is limited; they can only deal with so much.

A Narrow Face reveals less natural confidence. Narrow Face Individuals build confidence through life lessons, previous experience, acquired knowledge, or just plain hard work. Before attempting something new, they prefer to know as much as possible. When it comes to something about which they feel strongly, most tend to be confident. Many are independent spirits and know others may not always believe as they do.

A Narrow Face reveals heightened sensitivity. This gift can bring compassion, enhanced intuition, and creativity. But sensitivity can also be challenging because feelings are more easily felt. Bones showing on a face reveals pain has been deeply felt. A naturally Narrow Face Individual might put on weight so that he or she does not feel so much. With weight gain, a Narrow Face may no longer look as narrow.

If you have a partner with a Narrow Face, he or she is likely a sensitive being. Sensitive beings benefit from time alone, especially time spent in nature. You may feel no need to be alone and might feel rejected when your partner goes off for a time on his or her own. But if you, too, have a Narrow Face and are honest with yourself, you may desire to get away from time to time as well. Bring nature to your partner by putting a plant by the bed.

If you have a Narrow Face, thin skin, and delicate features, you are likely a highly sensitive person prone to sensory overload. If possible, lie down when you feel overwhelmed. Doing so will reduce stress so that you can rebalance and deal with things more effectively.

BASIC FACE SHAPES

The face shape frames the face. When reading a face, the face shape is not as important as the *facial features*. Face shapes provide basic information; features provide details. Read Section II in this book to learn about the features.

The basic shape reveals the basic character

Basic face shapes are Square, Round, and Triangular. Other recognizable face shapes are Rectangular, Oval, and Diamond. Many people have a face that is a combination of face shapes.

When determining a basic face shape note that it is rare for a face to be a perfect shape; however, a face may resemble a particular shape. For example, a Square Face is not likely to be a perfect square but will be about 90% square. The basic face shape reveals *general information about a person's nature*.

SQUARE FACE

A Square Face is square; it is a short face. Forehead and jawline are about the same width. Square Faces reveal confidence, steadiness, and stamina and are found on strong, practical, individuals. The Square Face is said to provide the foundation for "millionaire material"; much money can be made through persistence and hard work. Square Face Individuals tend to be tireless. Square Face Individuals who are not as ambitious can be happy with a steady income and stable family life. A Square Face suggests a thoughtful, stable, and trustworthy person.

Square Face

Round Face

Top Triangle Face

Bottom Triangle Face

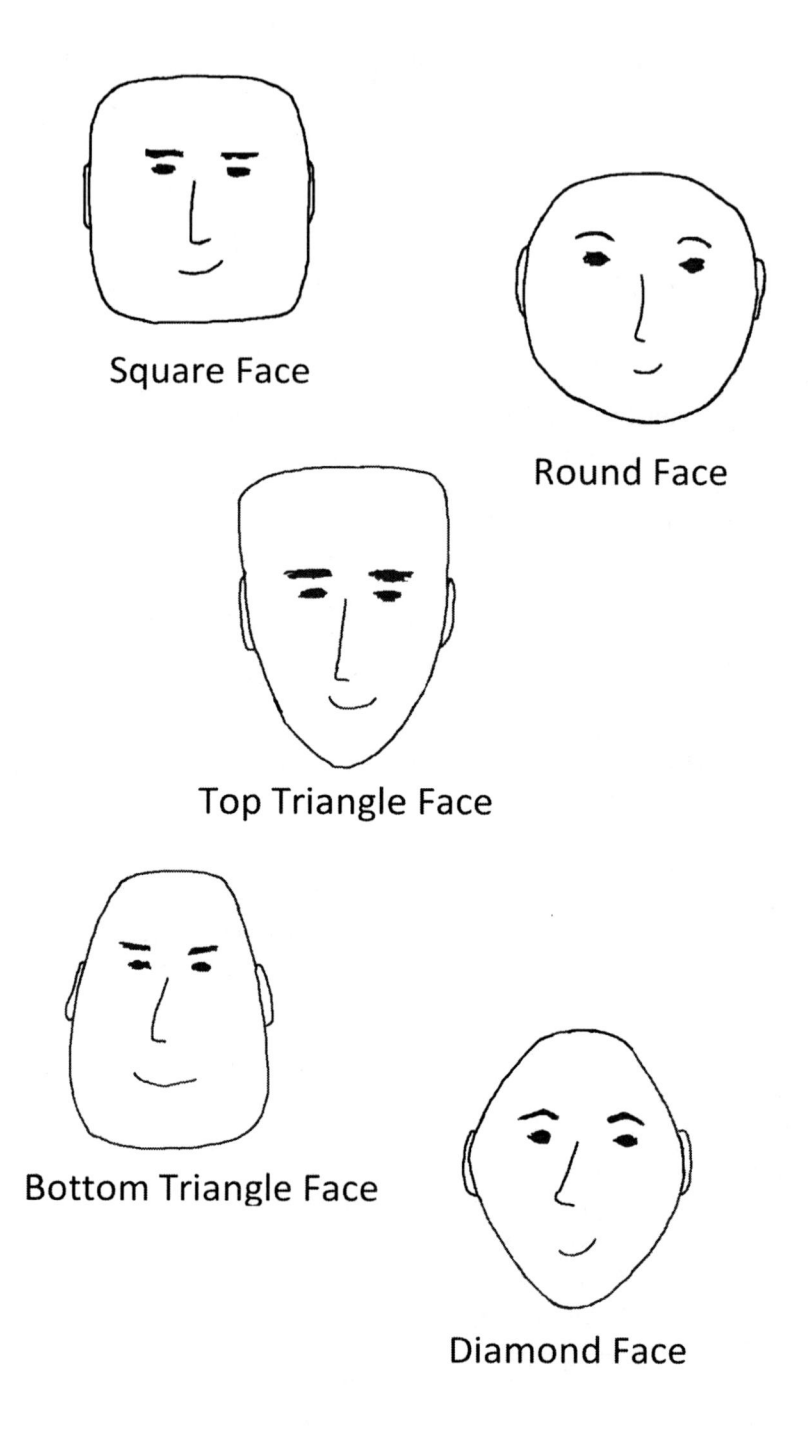

Diamond Face

Along with these gifts, there are potential challenges. A Square Face conveys stability; these individuals can be slow to move. They are not naturally flexible and may have difficulty with sudden changes over which they have no control. They can be quite stubborn and may be egotistical.

The sharper the corners, the more competitive and determined a Square Face Individual is likely to be. A slight *curve to the corners* adds softness and suggests more concern for others. This type of person will have a strong drive plus added diplomacy.

Square Face Individuals are most often sure of themselves and tend not to need validation from multiple people. For this reason, a Square Face Individual might find it easier than others to be in a monogamous relationship.

RECTANGULAR FACE

A Rectangular Face is a long squared shape. Many of the traits associated with a Square Face apply to a Rectangular Face but the length reveals more time is spent thinking before acting. Leaders of countries and businesses often have a Rectangular Face.

ROUND FACE

A Round Face is round in shape. Length and width are the same, and cheeks are full. This face shape reveals a gift for working with others. Round Face Individuals enjoy helping people feel important, appreciated, and cared for.

Round Faces have an open, friendly look that easily gains trust. Babies and puppies have round faces, as do many natural healers. Most Round Face Individuals have a people-oriented focus, but not all are as easy-going as perceived.

Round Faces suggest a down-to-earth nature and naturally cheery personality that most people find appealing and uplifting. They attract many friends and can excel in people-centered careers. The larger the facial features, the more ambitious a Round Face Individual will tend to be. One with a Round Face can be a hard worker, but will not do his or her best work when working nonstop. Having free time is important to them due to their social nature.

A Round Face that is *"irregularly round"* suggests a dealmaker with a gift for making a profit. A round shape tells of flexibility and adaptability and these gifts are enhanced when the face is *irregularly round*. Many with this face shape find success as brokers, financiers, salespeople, and entrepreneurs.

If dating a Round Face Individual, you may be gifted with one who sticks around when others might not. Round Face Individuals most often can be counted on when times are tough, while others might disappear, when you need them most. Round Face Individuals are naturally compassionate and adapt easily to changing circumstances. If you are dating a Round Face Individual who has been giving and caring, he or she will likely continue to be there for you in hard times.

OVAL FACE

An Oval Face is rounded with the forehead slightly wider than chin. Oval Face Individuals have many of the traits revealed in the Round Face, but have a more refined nature. They are not quite as open and are less spontaneous. An Oval Face suggests a heightened sense of manners and charm, gifts which can bring success in social relationships and business management. The Oval Face is a balanced face shape and tells of moderation.

TOP TRIANGLE FACE

A Top Triangle shape calls to mind a triangle with the horizontal part on top. This face is widest at the forehead and narrows to a pointed chin. A Top Triangle Face reveals expanding the mind is important to this individual.

Top Triangle Face Individuals are growth-oriented thinkers. They love to explore new ideas and are unhappy when confined in situations in which they do not have freedom. They don't take a job just for the money. These individuals "think" more than "do," which can create challenges when it comes to getting things done. This is especially true for those with long faces. The more pointed the chin, the more control issues they are likely to have. A Top Triangle Face Individual's strength is in thinking and planning.

Wide tops reveal a broad mental focus. *Very wide* tops suggest one who may be mentally aggressive. *The bigger the head*, the more an individual will want to be the authority. When the face is *narrower overall* it suggests a narrower intellectual focus and milder nature.

Top Triangle Individuals are often romantically inclined. When on a first date with one with this face shape, however, it may be wise to keep the topic focused on intellectual or technical topics until you establish common areas of interest.

A Top Triangle partner might develop his or her mind while neglecting his or her body. If this is the case, both the mind and the physique could expand over time.

BOTTOM TRIANGLE FACE

A Bottom Triangle Face bears a resemblance to a triangle with the base at the bottom. The face is slightly narrow at the forehead and widens at the jaw. A Bottom Triangle Face reveals an individual with a gift for taking action. Spending time in thought is not this individual's focus.

A face largest at the bottom reveals a physically based individual. Many of these individuals are gifted athletically. Bottom Triangle Face Individuals are action-oriented doers who focus on getting things done. They sometimes however, don't think enough before making a move. This is a potential challenge, as is narrow mindedness.

DIAMOND FACE

The Diamond Face is in a diamond shape. The cheekbones are wider than both the jaw and forehead. A Diamond Face shape reveals an individual who is talented in overcoming challenges and surmounting obstacles. These individuals are spirited with a competitive streak. They have a gift for innovation.

Diamond Face Individuals are motivated when they have a chance to outdo themselves or others. Money is important to Diamond Face Individuals, but not as critical as winning. They have an easier time reaching goals because reaching them is a priority. They require freedom in life, in relationships, and in work. Many enterprising individuals have a Diamond Face.

A Diamond Face suggests high standards and one inclined to be high strung. When these individuals want something, they want it immediately. They have a need to be noticed and a need to do things their way. *The broader the jaw*, the more physical stamina is revealed. *The broader the face*, the more confident a Diamond Face Individual is. An overly strong need to compete however, can reveal a deep-rooted lack of confidence, and jealousy is a potential challenge. One with a Diamond Face is also inclined to be impulsive.

If you want to get your Diamond Face partner to do something, tell him or her that he or she does not have the ability to do it.

Furthermore, a Diamond Face Individual will not be taken for granted. If your date has this face shape, acknowledgment is important if you would like to keep dating him or her. If your partner has this face shape, acknowledgment is important if you want harmony in your home.

Section II

THE DETAILS:

Reading Features

THE FEATURES

This section goes into detail about facial features. The Nose chapter, for example, discusses size, shape, bridge, nostrils and the gifts revealed. You may have only considered the nose in terms of breathing and smelling, but the nose also tells about a person's work-style, need for recognition, energy level, multi-tasking ability, and the desire to provide, protect, and save.

Each facial feature corresponds to one of the Five Chinese Elements. For example, ears correspond to the Water element. Although it is not necessary to know what element a feature corresponds to when doing a basic face reading, I have provided this information for those interested. More information on the Five Elements can be found in Section III.

All features provide valuable information about an individual's character, strengths, challenges, and gifts. However, there are five features that carry more weight than the others. These features are the ears, the eyebrows, the eyes, the nose, and the mouth. You may wish to pay more attention to these five major features.

THE EARS

Ears reveal courage, constitution, wisdom, attachment to family, and how a person handles risk. The need to stand out or fit in is revealed and ears also tell how a person listens. Ears correspond to the Water element.

High ears reveal high speed; low reveals slow

Examine whether ears are high set or low; how to judge this is described below. To obtain an accurate reading of ear placement, the face you are reading needs to be straight in front of you, at the same level as your face. If the face is tilted down, ears appear higher; likewise, if the face is tilted up, ears appear lower. In either case, the reading will not be accurate.

An alternate way to read ear placement is to view the face from the individual's profile. If you are looking at your own face, you will need both a hand mirror and a wall-mounted mirror to do this.

High Set Ears   Low Set Ears

Some ears are set high. Some ears are set low. Many fall in the mid-range. Placement of the ears reveals the *speed of listening and learning.*

HIGH SET EARS

When the top of the ear projects above the imaginary horizontal line level with the eyebrows, the ear is considered High Set. High Set Ears tell of a gift for quick listening and learning. These individuals often know what they want to do early in life. This gives them greater opportunity to become successful in their youth. High Set Ears show the intellect is activated quickly.

High Set Ears also stir up the mind. High Set Ears Individuals take in information instantly and handle it rapidly. They prefer a fast pace. They excel in situations that call for speed in dealing with information, but sometimes respond or take action before all information is received. Mistakes, mismatched replies, and unwise decisions might result. Impatience is a possible challenge.

If your partner has High Set Ears, he or she probably has a quick mind. If your ears are low, you are apt to handle information at a slower pace. Your partner with rapid processing may jump to conclusions or finish your sentences and might get annoyed if you repeat yourself. He or she heard what you said the first time.

If you are dating a High Set Ears Individual, you may find your date laughs at jokes that, to those with Low Set Ears, don't seem to make sense. This might embarrass you at first, if you don't hear the humor. The joke might make perfect sense, but Low Set Ears Individuals need time to think about it.

LOW SET EARS

When the top of the ear is below the imaginary line level with the outer corner of the eye, the ear is Low Set. Low Set Ears reveal listening and learning occurs at a slower pace. They suggest gifts of common sense and persistence. Low Set Ears Individuals process information slowly and carefully; they are patient listeners. And, patience may be needed in dealing with those with Low Set Ears.

Low Set Ears Individuals take their time. There is some stubbornness in those with this placement of ears. They will not be pushed into speeding up and would rather do something correctly than do something fast. When making decisions, they want to be sure they make the right decision and when listening, they want all facts.

Finding the right career or opportunity can take longer for Low Set Ears Individuals. They tend to take a while to discover their abilities and figure out what they want to do. However, time is not wasted, for they are busy gathering knowledge and perfecting skills for work that is just right. Wisdom gained from experience is often more valuable than knowledge at a young age. Learning is not always from books.

Some Low Set Ears Individuals do find their life's work early on in life. This work tends to be more physically than intellectually based or might be work using a creative talent such as singing.

Low Set Ears can indicate a turbulent childhood. Stability is important for Low Set Ears Individuals. They may be slow getting into a relationship, because they want to make sure it is the right relationship. Once they commit, they tend to be committed to making the relationship work.

Those with Low Set Ears often find success later in life. You may think your partner with Low Set Ears has not yet found his or her path. Each person has a unique path. Your partner is on his or hers.

Ears that stick out reveal a desire to stand out

Most people don't notice ears that are flat against the head as much as they notice ears that stick out. The ear body's distance from the head reveals a person's *desire to fit in or stand out*.

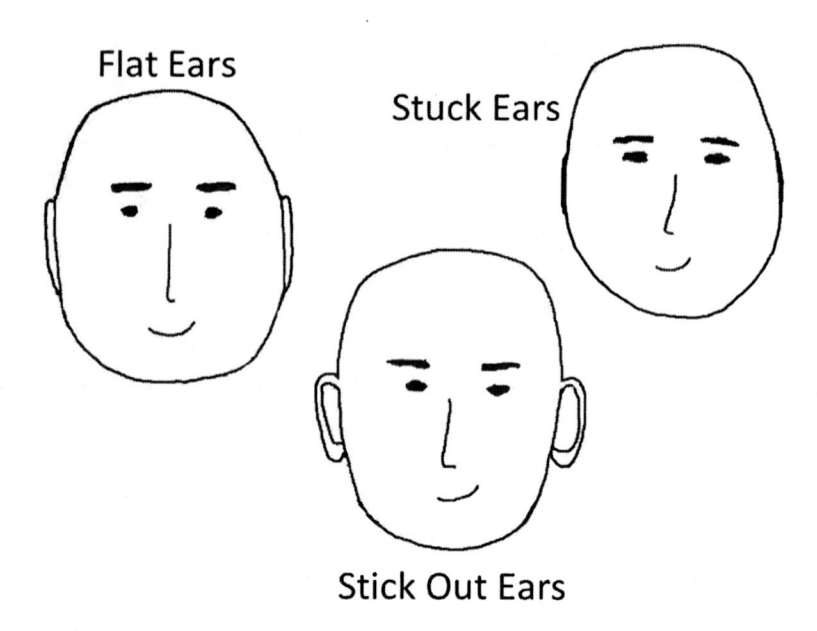

Flat Ears

Stuck Ears

Stick Out Ears

FLAT EARS

When there is little space between the ear's body and a person's head, the ear is flat to the head and is a Flat Ear. Flat Ears reveal a desire to fit in. These Individuals tend not to question too many things; they follow the rules and follow the trends. The more the ear "fits in" to the head, the more one desires to "fit in" with groups, family, society, and friends.

There are advantages to feeling accepted and belonging. Individuals relate to those like themselves and work well with those that get along. In school, students who fit in have an easier time being well liked and popular. The same is true in corporate culture. Fitting in bonds trust; indeed, salespeople can benefit from having Flat Ears. And, Flat Ears Individuals may have an easier time when travelling abroad. These ears can be advantageous as the world moves toward greater interdependence. Used wisely, Flat Ears are powerful.

Flat Ears suggest one who listens to and consider all sides. Flat Ears Individuals can excel in careers calling for their gift of polite listening, and these ears are beneficial when listening to family and friends. Ears that are *long*, as well as flat, suggest an individual who makes sound judgments.

A strong need to belong can be a Flat Ears Individual's potential challenge. Flat Ears Individuals need to be careful not to place more value on the opinions, ideas, and ideals of others than they do on their own.

A partner with Flat Ears may have an easier time conducting business in a foreign country. For example, after a meeting and a bite to eat, a man doing business in Finland might be asked to follow his clients into a brightly lit sauna as this is a cultural tradition. Although sweating naked with important clients may seem a bit weird to one not raised with this tradition, joining in is a way to fit in, bond, and gain trust, making it easier to sit naked in the unflattering light. Turning down the invitation to join in the sauna activity could seem antisocial to the clients and could negatively impact the business relationship.

You may have an easier time in a relationship with one with Flat Ears. A Flat Ears partner is likely to consider your way of thinking and listen to what you have to say. Around the house, you may be able to do many things your way. Be aware that Flat Ears also suggest a heightened sensitivity to manners. Things will flow more smoothly if you are appreciative, thankful, and considerate.

STUCK EARS

Stuck Ears are a variation of Flat Ears. When you look at a face from the front and can't see the ears, they are Stuck Ears. Stuck Ears are so flat to the head that they might appear to be stuck to it. These individuals have the gifts of Flat Ears as described above, but some additional challenges.

Stuck Ears tell of a very strong desire to fit in. Stuck Ears Individuals may conform routinely to the wishes of others and are often concerned with how they appear to others. Stuck Ears suggest that one is not living life to its fullest potential. *Large* Stuck Ears reveal one who has a better chance of taking a chance. A Stuck Ears Individual with *large* ears is more apt to break free and do something different than a person with *small* Stuck Ears. *Small* Stuck Ears Individuals can be rigid, making moving out of their comfort zone difficult.

A Stuck Ears Individual might not be fully aware of his or her desire to fit in to be like others. However, he or she may be conscious of the fact that when around outgoing people he or she is outgoing, and when around an introverted person he or she is more of an introvert.

If you have Stuck Ears you may habitually put needs of others ahead of your own. Being aware of this tendency may help you break free of this stuck pattern.

STICK OUT EARS

When an ear's body sticks out from the head it is a Stick Out Ear. Stick Out Ears Individuals have strong personalities; they tend to be stubborn, unconventional, and can be controversial. But, one with these ears has the potential to make a difference in the world by doing things differently.

Stick Out Ears Individuals have visionary potential and can bring about change. They do things in new ways. They are trendsetters; they have a gift for innovation; they have imagination and creativity. Still, for some, being different might also mean isolation, alienation, and the challenge of being misunderstood. Stick Out Ears reveal a desire to stand out.

Stick Out Ears indicate a rebellious nature. They don't have the easiest time taking advice from others. Rebellious individuals often know what is best for them and listen to this inner knowing. On some individuals Stick Out Ears also tilt forward. The more the ears tilt forward, the more one is closed to hearing the opinions of others. These individuals love listening to their own voice!

Stick Out Ears Individuals can find compromise challenging. These ears suggest defiance. At times, a Stick Out Ears Individual might need to take care, so as not to appear rude.

When a Stick Out Ears Individual prefers to cover his or her ears with hair or a hat, this can mean he or she is not entirely comfortable being different. If the hair style or hat is unusual however, this increases the likelihood of standing out and these individuals are aware of this. And, when Stick Out Ears are exposed on a shaved head or seen on one whose hair is pulled back, this suggests an individual who is at ease standing out and who might want to call attention to him- or herself.

You may have Flat Ears and a partner with Stick Out Ears. If you suggest your partner do something because "Everyone is doing it," your partner is likely to respond, "And that is why I am not!"

When engaged in a discussion with a Stick Out Ears Individual, be aware of selective hearing. A person with these ears is apt to pick up only that which aligns with his or her way of thinking. With selective hearing, a Stick Out Ears Individual has an opinion, and ears that are not always receptive to your ideas.

Perhaps you have just started dating an individual with Stick Out Ears. These individuals tend to follow the beat of a different drummer. Your date may have a quirky uniqueness that you find attractive, but others find odd. If you, too, have always followed your own drum beat, the relationship could work due to the "outside the ordinary" bond you share. But, if your Stick Out Ears date feels left out because of being so far out, he or she may rebel against being different. In an attempt to try to fit in, he or she might seek a partner who looks and acts more like everyone else.

A strong desire to fit in is more prevalent in younger individuals due to peer pressure. Age brings awareness of the gifts of Stick Out Ears.

Size suggests listening ability and how hearing is handled

There is no absolute measurement that defines a long, large, or small ear. When determining ear size, compare ears with the size of the head. Ears seem to have gotten smaller over the years. Very Large Ears are seen less in modern times than in years past. Ear size reveals *length of listening ability* and *desire to listen to others*.

Large Ears

Long Ears

Small Ears

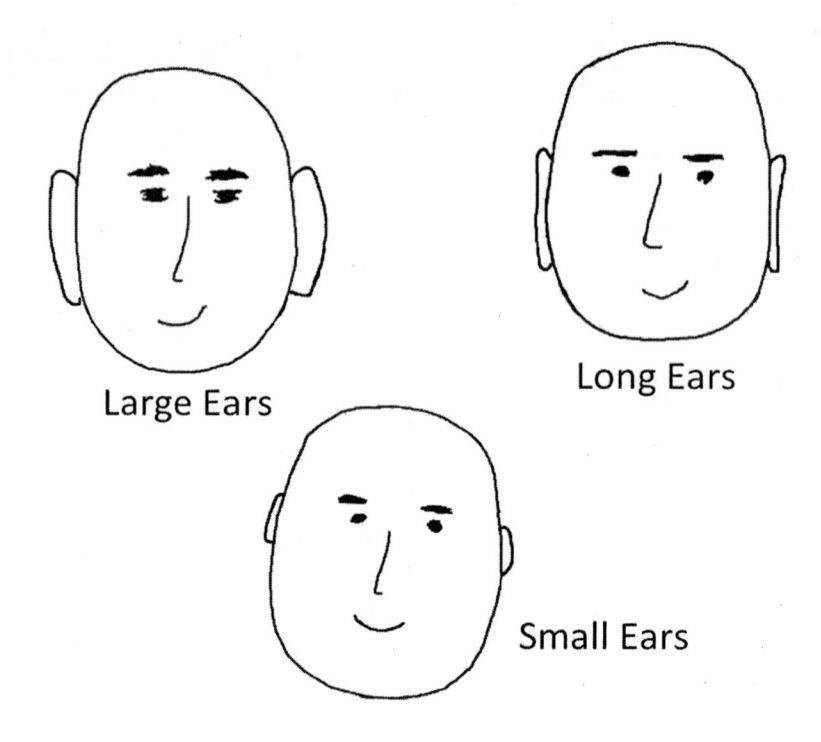

LONG EARS

Long Ears reveal the gifts of the ability to listen for a long time and the desire to listen to others. They suggest a more intellectual than intuitive nature.

Long Ears Individuals most often listen well and thus tend to make good listeners. They are less likely than smaller eared individuals to get tired or cranky from auditory overload. Therapists, counselors, courtroom judges, and those handling complaints in customer service benefit from having Long Ears. Long Ears individuals may benefit from the wisdom of others; indeed, Long Ears suggest one with the patience to listen to helpful suggestions from friends.

There are challenges that come from long, patient listening. Decisions take more time due to the need to hear and consider everything first and kind individuals with Long Ears let talkative friends talk on and on. A Long Ears Individual might spend too much time listening when he or she needs to be doing other things.

A Long Ears date might be a good listener but may take a while to respond.

Your partner with Long Ears may have no problem sitting through long movies with more talking than action, but if you have Small Ears, this may not be easy for you to endure.

LARGE EARS

Large Ears are both broad and long. They are proportionately large in relation to the head. Large Ears indicate the gift of a strong constitution, providing an advantage for health and longevity. Because Large Ears are long, they bring long listening ability and a natural desire to listen. Listening to others is considered an act of kindness; individuals with long or Large Ears are often thought of as kind.

Outgoing and enterprising, Large Ears Individuals are blessed with good business sense and a desire to take responsibility. They make strong leaders. The broadness in their ears reveals courage. Large Ears with *long earlobes* suggest wisdom and long life.

Your Large Ears partner is likely to have an abundance of energy. Large Ears Individuals often can burn the candle at both ends without negative effects. Still, over time they may need to watch for burnout. To determine if your partner needs to take better care of him- or herself, check the ear's cartilage. You might feel the ears while kissing or fondle them while watching a film or television. A firm feel indicates energy is good. A flimsy feel suggests that strength is waning and more rest would be best.

SMALL EARS

Small Ears reveal a gift for handling auditory information quickly and easily, a gift enhanced when the ears are set high. Small Ears Individuals tend not to desire to listen for a long time.

Small Ears Individuals listen and process information rapidly and do best when information is also visual. They tire from too much time listening and do what they can to speed things up; they don't always wait (or want) to hear all details or facts. They can find it difficult listening to others' problems, thoughts, or opinions.

Small Ears tell of an intuitive nature. This can play a part in Small Ears Individuals not wanting to listen. Often they "just know" things. Small Ears are also good for picking up the subtleties of sounds.

Small Ears with *smooth, well-formed rims* suggest an appreciation of beautiful surroundings and possible artistic talents. Small Ears with *irregularly shaped rims* often reveal a rough beginning in life.

If you have a partner with *thin or delicate* Small Ears, you may find he or she has quick bursts of energy but might need a nap from time to time. By honoring your partner's need for renewal, you will have a better chance of having your partner around later in life or at least a better chance of having an energetic partner later in the evening.

If you have started dating a Small Ears Individual with ears *set high*, be alert to quick responses that don't make sense. Small Ears Individuals are not the best listeners and those with ears *set high* often respond before hearing all the facts. Also be aware of a Small Ears Individual's need for recognition. If not received, he or she is likely to become depressed.

The shape of the ear affects what one hears

Ears come in different shapes. They can be rounded, straight, or pointy. Often ears have no clear shape or are a combination of shapes. And some individuals have very unique looking ears that are shaped oddly. Ear shape reveals *how one listens*.

(NOTE: For illustration purposes, ears are drawn sticking out. Actual ears may stick out or may lie flat to the head.)

FACE READING FOR LOVE

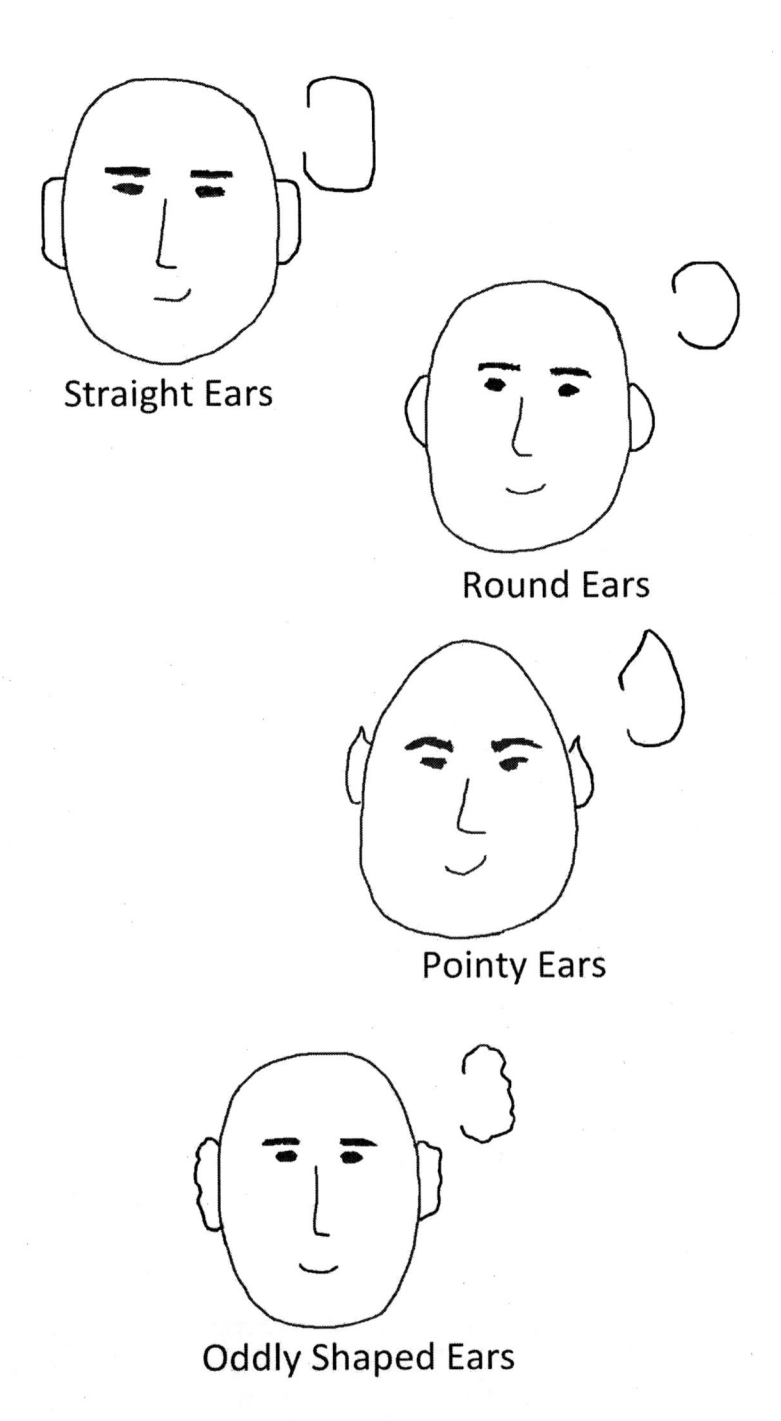

Straight Ears

Round Ears

Pointy Ears

Oddly Shaped Ears

ROUND EARS

An ear with a rounded outer edge is a Round Ear. Round Ears are people-centered ears. These individuals listen with an interest in others, have a gift for harmonious relationships, and excel in people-focused careers. Round Ears might also tell of a natural gift for music.

Accuracy for sound is found in ears very round. Round Ears suggest sensitivity to rhythm; a trait enhanced when ears are *delicate*. Those with *delicate* Round Ears often can feel music physically. Feeling plays a part, too, when listening to others, because the rounder the edge, the more the individual listens from the heart than the head.

If your partner has *large, sturdy, thick-rimmed* Round Ears, this suggests he or she is energized by people and music. If your partner has *small, delicate, thin-rimmed* Round Ears, this suggests he or she likes people and *deeply feels* music but can easily become fatigued around too many people or too much music.

You may find that a date with Round Ears cares about what you have to say. Look to the ears' length and the rims' thickness for clues on how long he or she may want to listen.

STRAIGHT EARS

An ear with a straight outer edge is a Straight Ear. Straight Ears reveal outside-the-box thinking. These individuals listen with an ear for what they need to hear.

Straight Ears suggest independent spirits with a gift for doing things in new and different ways. To use this gift they need to be in charge, self-employed, or have flexibility in the work they do. They are easily frustrated, impatient, or unproductive when held back. They find it challenging working for others. Some Straight Ears are straight on the top, the lobe, and the side. When one has such *squared* ears, this suggests a sharp-minded individual with a gift for leadership.

Straight Ears Individuals listen for what they feel is important and cut out the rest when listening. They tend to ignore what they consider unnecessary, uninteresting, or not to be believed. This keeps them focused and helps them get things done.

When speaking to your partner, you may speak clearly and directly, but if your partner has Straight Ears, he or she may not always hear everything. Blame the ears. Your partner may not be aware he or she is not listening fully.

If you have recently started dating someone with Straight Ears, he or she may not hear all you have to say, because what you are sharing is of little or no interest to him or her. If your date is of interest to you, try changing to a topic you both find interesting. But, if what you are talking about is more important to you than the date to whom you are talking, you may wish to find someone else.

POINTY EARS

An ear with a pointy tip on top is a Pointy Ear. Pointy Ears Individuals listen with an ear for excitement. Although ears correspond to the Water element, the Fire element is revealed in the pointy tip. These individuals have a fiery personality.

Pointy Ears Individuals are drawn to adventure and interesting people and sometimes create drama to stimulate things. These ears suggest erotic sensuality. Pointy Ears reveal an original, inventive, and imaginative individual; you won't be bored with this person.

Pointy Ears also suggest a sharp mind. Enchanting and clever, these individuals can devise answers to problems quickly or come up with a "story" when necessary. Pointy Ears Individuals may have challenges when it comes to their behavior, which is known to be unpredictable and impulsive. It may take a sharp mind to understand them; Pointy Ears Individuals are difficult to figure out.

Pointy Ears often reveal an individual who grew up in a chaotic household. These ears show a strong possibility of childhood trauma, and emotions can become volatile when a Pointy Ears person is afraid. They have a tendency to be reactive and often have control issues. Their ears are highly tuned to sudden changes; in their past, they may have needed to move quickly.

Pointy Ears Individuals are accustomed to action and don't like being bored. This can bring up challenges when attempting to settle down.

When earlobes are long and fleshy, this adds grounding and purpose, increasing the possibility of committing to a relationship, but decreasing a Pointy Ears person's mysterious charm.

Your Pointy Ears potential partner may talk of seeking stability. An exciting life, however, is not easily given up. True feelings about commitment may be kept a mystery. Your Pointy Ears companion might be cleverly charming you.

ODDLY SHAPED EARS

Oddly Shaped Ears are formed peculiarly and tell of an erratic beginning. When rims look mangled, this reveals early trauma likely played a part in an individual's life. Bumps and indentations appearing along the outer rims' *inner edge* are further indications that early years (conception to age 14) did not go smoothly. Oddly Shaped Ears Individuals listen in unpredictable ways.

Individuals with Oddly Shaped Ears have the challenge of making the best of a less-than-positive start. Some people with a bad start make life difficult for others. When an Oddly Shaped Ears Individual's eyes are bright, steady, and clear and his or her face radiates warmth, it reveals the gift of inner strength and suggests a rough beginning has been, or is being, overcome.

A partner with Oddly Shaped Ears might find it challenging giving and receiving love. The core of all individuals is good, but individuals with these ears are often hindered by a childhood that wasn't.

Slant suggests outlook

Viewing the face from profile, ears may be vertical or may slant back. Assess slant by drawing an imaginary line from the center of the earlobe to the center of the top of the ear. If the line is vertical, it is a Vertical Ear. If the ear is not vertical, but slants back, it is a Slanted Ear. The ears' slant tells of an individual's *outlook on life*.

Vertical Ear

Slanted Ear

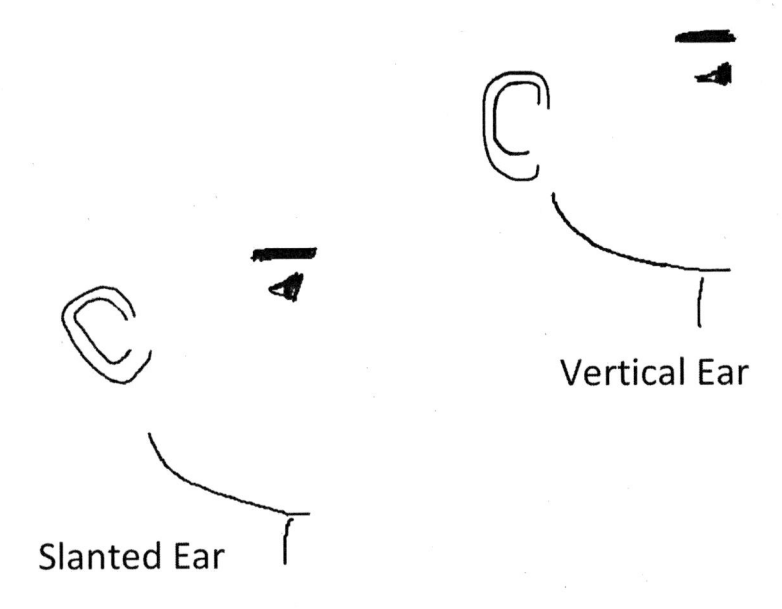

VERTICAL EARS

Vertical Ears reveal a logical outlook and a levelheaded approach. Vertical Ears Individuals tend to be comfortable with the established way of thinking. Others can relate to them and this helps gain assistance in getting things done.

A Vertical Ears partner is more likely to go along with the status quo than an individual who has ears that slant back. He or she might say, "If something is working, it doesn't need to be fixed."

SLANTED EARS

Slanted Ears Individuals have a unique outlook and perspective. Because of their atypical take on life, their challenge might be in getting others to understand their point of view. Their strength is in doing things differently. This gift can bring about change.

Width reveals risk taking

The width of an ear tells of courage and the desire to take risks. The entire ear may be narrow or broad, or only one section may have noticeable width. The bigger the ear, the easier it is for an individual to take chances. Ear width reveals *comfort in taking risks.*

Note that ears as discussed below refer to the ear's *body* and not the *earlobe*. Earlobes tell of future-type risks and are described in the following section.

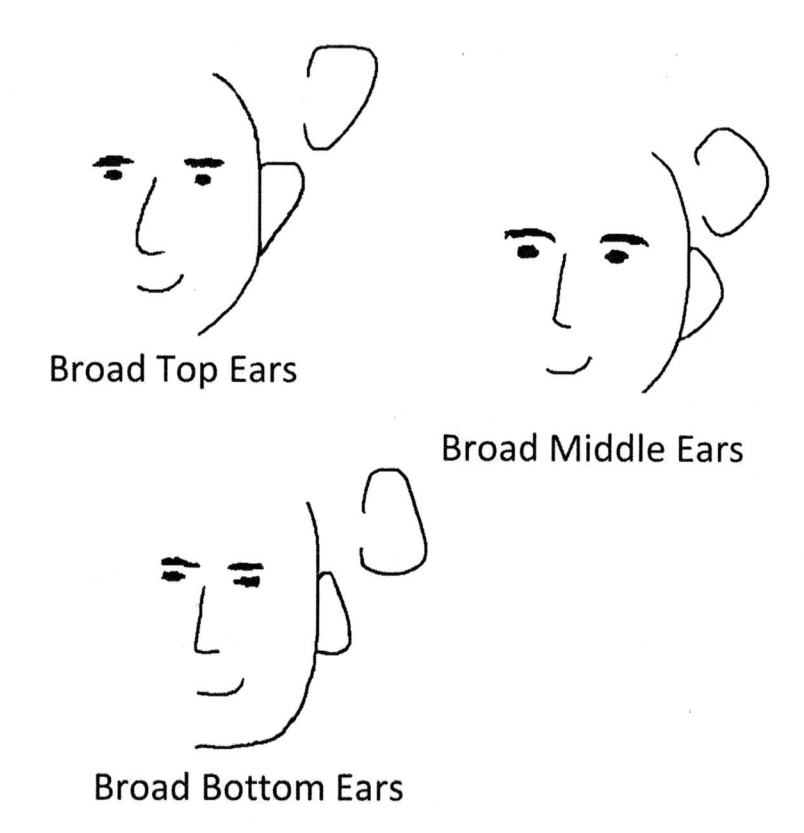

Broad Top Ears

Broad Middle Ears

Broad Bottom Ears

BROAD EARS

When the entire ear is broad, it is a Broad Ear. Broad Ears indicate an expansive approach to life. These individuals are comfortable taking all types of risks and most are thrill-seekers of one form or another. The bigger the ear, the more courageous a person is likely to be.

Broad Ears Individuals tend not to hesitate to try something new, giving them greater opportunity to live life to its fullest potential. When *large* Broad Ears *stick out* from the side of the head, this suggests a fearless individual. Impulsive or unwise risk taking are potential challenges for Broad Ears Individuals.

NARROW EARS

An ear that is narrow along its entire length is a Narrow Ear. Narrow Ears tell of a desire for safety and security. These Individuals are not naturally comfortable taking risks. Careful caution is the gift; risks taken tend to be small and thought out. Those who are overly cautious, however, miss opportunities. Some with Narrow Ears just put up with things the way they are.

If your partner has Narrow Ears, risky behavior is not in his or her nature. Although at times you might wish your partner would risk more, the benefits of having a partner who risks less means less chance you will have to worry about your partner getting involved in dicey financial ventures, unwise sexual escapades, or speeding with kids in the car.

BROAD TOP EARS

Ears broad only on top are Broad Top Ears. They suggest comfort in intellectual or financial risks. Broad Top Ears Individuals may be successful running their own business or working for commission-based pay. Working this way is energizing to them.

Your partner with Broad Top Ears may have no fear taking risks concerning money matters. But, if money matters to you, your partner's risk-taking may be your concern.

NARROW TOP EARS

Ears narrow only in the top section are Narrow Top Ears. These ears reveal a person not comfortable taking mental or financial risks. When it comes to work, most prefer a steady job and steady paycheck.

If single and seeking an individual who is not likely to have a gambling problem, look for someone with Narrow Top Ears. Financial caution is even more likely if the ears are also *small*.

BROAD MIDDLE EARS

Ears broad only across the middle section are Broad Middle Ears. Broad Middle Ears reveal comfort in taking emotional risks.

Broad Middle Ears Individuals tend not to let fear get in the way of doing what needs to be done. They have a gift for taking emotional risks in order to live the life they want to live. Problems might arise when risks are impulsive.

If you are eager to be in a relationship, you may want to check out the width of the ears. Broad Middle Ears suggest an individual who has an easier time taking a risk on a relationship. Narrowness here suggests hesitancy.

NARROW MIDDLE EARS

Ears narrow only across the middle section are Narrow Middle Ears. Narrow Middle Ears reveal individuals who are not comfortable taking

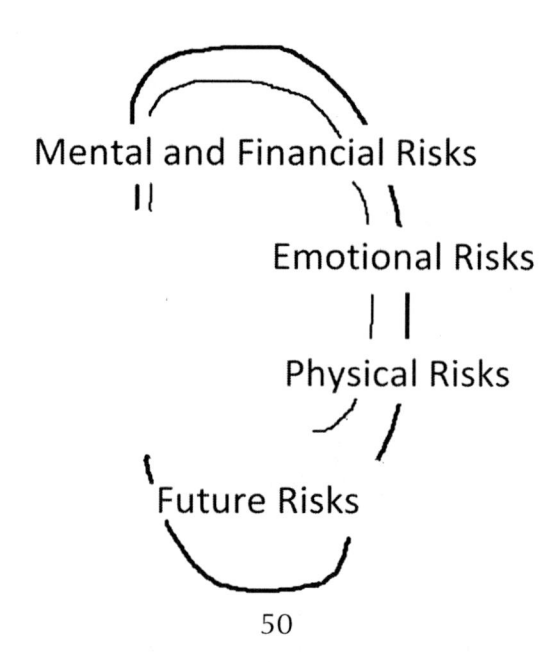

Mental and Financial Risks

Emotional Risks

Physical Risks

Future Risks

emotional risks. Intelligent caution is the gift; it allows them to give careful thought to potentially harmful situations.

An individual with Narrow Middle Ears will give considerable thought before committing to, or ending, a relationship.

BROAD BOTTOM EARS

Ears broad only across the lower ear section are Broad Bottom Ears. They tell of physical courage and suggest one energized by taking physical risks. Dangerous careers such as working as a rescue helicopter pilot in a fire or war zone might suit one with Broad Bottom Ears. Extreme sports or hard-core adventure travel may be found appealing.

A partner with *large* Broad Bottom Ears that *stick out* might live to test his or her physical abilities in ways that frighten you. It is natural for an extremely physical risk-taking person to push physical boundaries in situations where one might not survive. Living on the edge makes these daring individuals feel more alive. Although some see taking such risks as a "death wish," it is actually a "life wish" that many of these individuals have.

NARROW BOTTOM EARS

When the lower portion of the ear is exceptionally narrow, it is a Narrow Bottom Ear. Narrow Bottom Ears reveal a physically cautious nature and one not comfortable with physical risks. Their caution brings less chance of getting hurt, but can also mean less chance of having fun. These individuals "physically feel" fear more easily than most. Narrow Bottom Ears Individuals desire to keep their body safe and secure.

If you take a Narrow Bottom Ears date to an amusement park, stick to slower rides that stay close to the ground. Unless, that is, you find it amusing to watch your date become frightened. And, if your date sees that you find it entertaining to see him or her get scared, it might be your last date.

Earlobes show stability and appreciation for the material world

Earlobe size relates to the earlobe's length, width, and thickness. You may need to observe several different ears before you can distinguish the size of earlobes. Earlobe size reveals *physical grounding and comfort taking future-type risks.*

BROAD EARLOBES

Broad Earlobes tell of appreciation of the physical aspects of life. Those with Broad Earlobes may have a gift for growing money and may also be good at growing plants. These lobes reveal a large storehouse of inherent energy and those who are grounded. These individuals tend to be comfortable taking long-term or future-type risks. Investing in real estate is an example of a long-term risk that would appeal to a Broad Earlobes Individual.

NARROW EARLOBES

Narrow Earlobes reveal individuals more present oriented than future oriented. Tending to prefer instant gratification, they might have challenges when it comes to long-term financial planning or taking future-type risks. If Narrow Earlobes are *long*, this adds some grounding and conventional wisdom and adds to their desire or ability to save.

A Narrow Earlobes Individual tends to live in the moment. Living in the moment is also known as living in the now, which is considered by many enlightened individuals to be the true path to happiness. When thinking this way, living in the moment may be wise.

LONG EARLOBES

Long Earlobes reveal a gift for future planning and one comfortable taking a long-term or future-type risk. When *plump* or *fleshy*, these lobes indicate vitality and the potential for a long life. Longevity provides more time to work and grow savings and more time for wisdom to develop. Long Earlobes suggest an individual who is physically grounded in the world.

Wisdom, a combination of knowledge and understanding, most often comes later in life. When earlobes are very long, they are said to reveal spiritual wisdom. However, one who is spiritually wise often has less concern about living long or accumulating wealth.

Wearing heavy earrings can lengthen earlobes, but the earlobes will become thinner and less fleshy. They will become *delicate* earlobes. Although the earlobes' length will increase, the above gifts may be reduced.

A partner with naturally Long Earlobes may be very good at managing retirement savings. In future years, you may appreciate your partner's wise investing.

SHORT EARLOBES

Short Earlobes reveal a more metaphysical than physical orientation to life and a shorter supply of innate life force energy, which in Chinese Medicine is known as Jing. Those who take care, however, can live a long time. Short Earlobes suggest one less grounded in the physical world.

Short Earlobes Individuals can be impulsive and may be challenged when planning and saving for the future; things they tend to dislike. But those spiritually based may feel no need to do so. They trust all their needs will be met. Others of a different mindset might need to play catch-up later on.

A Short Earlobes partner is likely to want to spend money on what is needed, or desired, in the moment. A Long Earlobes partner may prefer to save for what might be needed in the future.

NO LOBES

Some earlobes are angled and look as if they are "cut off." Angled earlobes can be termed No Lobes.

No Lobes suggest a physically cautious individual. This is especially true when No Lobes are on *small ears*. You are not likely to see this person doing complex skateboard tricks, jumping out of planes, or hang-gliding off cliffs. Although they do not desire to be up in the air physically, a No Lobes Individual might have trouble staying grounded.

No Lobes can reveal a curious individual. An inquisitive nature is the gift; interested individuals don't get bored. No Lobes also tell of intuition. Yet, these individuals have a questioning nature and often ask for advice from others. No Lobes Individuals many times already have the answers they seek from others; they often just need to believe in themselves more.

And, No Lobes reveal strong *emotional* ties to family. No Lobes are a form of Attached Earlobes. Read more about Attached Earlobes in the section that follows.

Your partner with No Lobes is likely an inquisitive individual whose curious questioning may be irritating at times for it may go on and on. No Lobes Individuals have a nature that wants to know. But if you partner asks, and you don't know, respond to the question by just saying so. The questioning will then have nowhere to go.

PLUMP EARLOBES

When earlobes are fleshy and full, they are Plump Earlobes. Plump Earlobes reveal a sturdy nature and a person who finds pleasure in material things.

Plump Earlobes suggest a healthy constitution, a strong physical base, and one who might enjoy activities such as hiking or gardening. These earlobes suggest a grounded, stable individual. Plump Earlobes also reveal a desire to accumulate money. Earthy in nature, when it comes to taking future-type risks, Plump Earlobes Individuals may be quite comfortable with land-based investments.

THICK DANGLING EARLOBES

When long earlobes hang down and are thick they are Thick Dangling Earlobes. Thick Dangling Earlobes suggest money comes easily. Easy money may come from the lottery, inheritance, settlements, or presents. But these lobes tell of a possible challenge when it comes to managing money. Without caution, easy money is easily spent. Financial planning tends not to be these individuals' strength or interest.

Earlobes large and *thick but not dangling* suggest a self-assured, goal-oriented individual. This individual may need to work harder for money, but will have an easier time hanging on to it.

DELICATE EARLOBES

Soft, thin earlobes are Delicate Earlobes; they tell of a delicate nature and one likely less grounded. Delicate Earlobes suggest limited energy and less desire to do lots of physical things.

For these individuals, financial planning tends not to be a priority. These lobes suggest less interest and less comfort in future-type risks. These earlobes instead suggest a romantic nature and refined mind. Delicate Earlobes reveal heightened sensitivity and the challenge to use that gift wisely.

Delicate Earlobes Individuals benefit from a calm environment. Loud noises, loud voices, and rough acting individuals can easily stress them out. Extra sensitivity can bring more emotionality, scattering energy and drawing on energy from already reduced reserves.

Delicate Earlobes suggest less attachment to a material sense of existence, allowing the mind to expand more easily beyond what is seen. Often a Delicate Earlobes Individual is a spiritual individual. However, others with these lobes need some grounding as they tend to live in fantasy.

EARLOBE HOLES

Although worn by indigenous cultures throughout time, gauges in recent times have become trendy. A gauge is a disk inserted into an earlobe after it has been pierced. A gauge stretches the earlobe, and over time, wearing larger sized gauges creates larger and larger holes. Those who wear gauges usually wear them in both ears.

As noted, the earlobe tells of physical grounding and reveals the level of comfort in taking future-type risks. Long-term investments are typical future-type risks.

Getting Earlobe Holes can be a future risk; wearing gauges might decrease the opportunity to make money that could be saved. Large gauges in large Earlobe Holes can bring challenges when it comes to career. Not all employers are open to this opening.

Large Earlobe Holes suggest the possibility of being less grounded. Large Earlobe Holes might bring about a "spacy" feeling or sense of emptiness. However, the sturdier the overall face, especially in the lower portion, the less likely this will be the case.

Those with Earlobe Holes who stretched their lobes before others followed the trend are rebellious by nature and have a desire to stand out. Those who wear ear gauges after they have become common and popular are those who desire to fit in. These individuals want to be accepted by others or at least by their friends. Rather than being trendsetters, they follow the trends.

Large gauges in your date's ears may be a turn-off or a turn-on. At least you get this information up front, unlike body jewelry worn on private parts.

Lobe attachment tells of a desire to remain attached

The way the earlobe connects to the face indicates if it is attached or detached. Earlobe attachment reveals *attachment to family of origin* or *attachment to the family in which one was raised*.

FACE READING FOR LOVE

Attached Earlobe

No space

Detached Earlobe

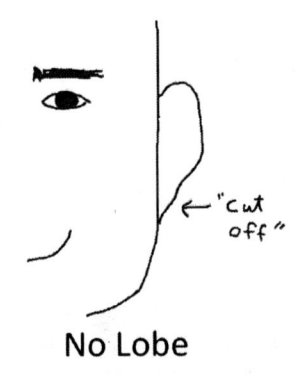

Space

No Lobe

"Cut off"

ATTACHED EARLOBES

When there is *no space* between the earlobe and the side of the face, the earlobe is an Attached Earlobe. Attached Earlobes suggest difficulty un-attaching from the influence of family of origin or the family in which one was raised.

Individuals with Attached Earlobes may move away physically, but stay connected emotionally, although family relations may not always be harmonious. The gift is the strong bond to family. The challenge is a strong desire for approval.

An Attached Earlobe that angles in toward the face, appearing to be "cut off," is a *No Lobe* earlobe. Information on No Lobes may be found in the previous section.

Your partner with Attached Earlobes may not be on good terms with parents or siblings for good reasons that you *may* understand. What you *may not* understand is why your partner says he or she doesn't care what they think but never stops thinking about them, asking for their advice, or trying to impress them.

DETACHED EARLOBES

When an earlobe hangs down below where it connects on the face, there is a *space*, making it a Detached Earlobe. Detached Earlobes reveal less desire to stay connected to one's family of origin or family in which one was raised. Those with Detached Earlobes have an easier time distancing themselves from family influence.

Once out of the house, Detached Earlobes Individuals make their own decisions. Some move far away; others stay close, but are indifferent about maintaining a connection. Detached Earlobes Individuals are often closer to friends than family. Some have no need for friends or family at all and are comfortable being alone. The gift of Detached Earlobes is that progress in life may be faster due to not being held back by parents or siblings.

If your partner has Detached Earlobes, he or she has the emotional detachment needed to move forward with his or her life.

Circles reveal inner or outer listening

An Ear has an outside rim and an inner ridge. In many people one will be more prominent. Although more like the form of a semi-circle, for face reading purposes the outside rim can be termed the Outer Circle and the inner ridge can be termed the Inner Circle. Ear Circles reveal *objective or subjective listening.*

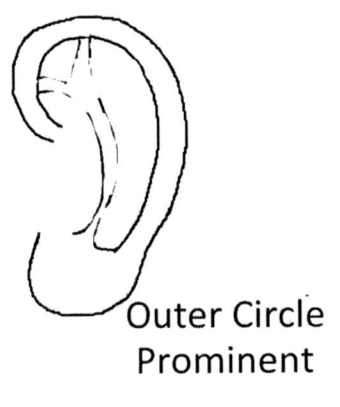

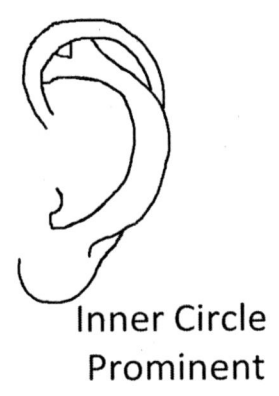

Outer Circle Prominent

Inner Circle Prominent

OUTER CIRCLE PROMINENT

When the outside rims are thick and well-defined, and inner ridges flat or unclear, ears are Outer Circle Prominent. Outer Circle Prominent Individuals place trust in logic and facts; their focus is on people, places, and things. Their interest tends to be more on the surface of life. Outside focused, they don't always listen to or express their inner feelings. Actually, they may not be fully aware of them.

Outer Circle Prominent Individuals are most often straightforward. They have gifts of common sense and reason; emotions don't easily throw them off balance. They focus on the objective side of listening. When outside rims are *very thick* this reveals one who may indulge in food or sex.

Outer Circle Prominent Individuals often live life for the benefit of the outer self, at least in their younger years. Interest in spiritual matters may not develop until later in life.

A partner with Outer Circle Prominent ears might have an advanced degree because he or she thinks it is just common sense to have one. It brings financial rewards and tends to impress others.

INNER CIRCLE PROMINENT

When inner ridges are very noticeably raised, or if they stick out beyond the ears' border, the ears are Inner Circle Prominent. Those with Inner Circle Prominent ears place trust in their feelings and beliefs. These ears suggest subjective listening; intuition plays a big part in what they hear. Inner Circle Prominent Individuals often have a deep desire to understand the meaning of life. They tend to be more interested in the inner workings of a person's mind than in the outer work a person does. Inner Circle Prominent Individuals are strong personalities who tend not to hold back when expressing themselves.

Inner Circle Prominent Individuals are natural non-conformists. They look for adventure, new people, exciting work, and interesting things. Many are creative types. Musicians, writers, artists, inventors, and mystics often have Inner Circle Prominent ears.

Because Inner Circle Prominent Individuals listen to their intuition, they know what is right for them. They can be stubborn when it comes to sticking to their feelings and beliefs. If your partner is Inner Circle Prominent he or she may view life in a way that you can't see. You might at times feel he or she is being difficult.

The feeling of the firmness reveals the firmness of the feelings

When grasping the ears and moving them back and forth, they may be difficult to move or they may bend easily. In determining firmness, you need to physically feel the ears. Ear hardness or softness is not seen easily; it must be felt. Ear firmness reveals *the degree of flexibility in an individual's nature.*

HARD EARS

Ears firm, rigid, or stiff are Hard Ears. They suggest tough, hard-headed characters. Once a Hard Ears Individual makes up his or her mind, it is difficult to get him or her to change it. These individuals can get stuck in their ways and often have difficulty accepting the ways of others. Hard Ears reveal the gift of determined persistence but also the challenges of inflexibility and lack of tolerance.

Hard Ears reveal driven individuals. Used wisely, their drive can help them reach goals and bring success. However, Hard Ears Individuals tend to be hard on themselves, which can be hard on their health; their rigidity can be difficult for others.

A Hard Ears Individual is likely to enjoy listening to louder music with a heavier beat than one with *delicate* ears with a preference for softer, more refined sounds. If your partner with Hard Ears is listening to loud music and a person with delicate ears asks your partner to turn the music down, if fixed on the music, your partner may stubbornly resist.

SOFT EARS

Ears soft and flexible are Soft Ears. They suggest one who is flexible, agreeable, and accommodating. Things tend to be negotiable with those who have Soft Ears. Soft Ears indicate one open to hearing the thoughts and opinions of others; but also one who may be swayed by others. Challenges for them are hesitancy, a potential to wavier, and caring too much about other's opinions.

Soft Ears also indicate lower vitality. *Flimsy* Soft Ears reveal strength is waning, and it's time to take a break. Soft Ears Individuals might have an agreeable nature in part due to lack of energy to get into a fight, an argument, or debate.

You may be uncertain where your Soft Ears partner stands on a certain issue. Whatever you partner's opinion was on the topic, talk to him or her tomorrow and the opinion is likely to have changed.

A person's ears can become softer when he or she cares too much what others think. Life essence is being used up when this happens. If you have Soft Ears you may be interested in knowing this. And if your ears are not soft you, too, may find this information of value.

Very red suggests the heart rules the head

Ears are normally a lighter color than the rest of the face, and earlobes usually have more color than the rest of the ear. Dark or thick skin decreases the likelihood of seeing a red or pale ear. Ear color reveals *passion*.

RED EARS

Ears are not normally red, but earlobes are often pinkish. Red Ears reveal an emotional, excitable individual with thin skin. Passion is revealed, and this gives purpose to life. But Red Ears Individuals also tend to have their feelings hurt easily. Red Ears suggest that one is ruled more by the heart than by the head.

When only the inner ridge of the left ear is red, or if this part of the left ear is itching, this indicates an individual is not listening to his- or her inner self. Such a message needs to be heeded.

PALE EARS

Ears are normally lighter than the rest of the face, but when they appear much lighter, they are Pale Ears. Pale Ears indicate reduced vitality and a lower level of passion. This may be a person's nature or may be only a temporary condition. Eating blood-building foods (examples are grapes and beef) might help as will more rest. Lack of passion might be due to uninteresting work or an uninspiring love life. Change might be needed, but there may be lack of energy to make a change. If a Pale Ears person tells you he or she is tired, believe him or her.

Lost hair from the head might be found in the ears

Hair grows in some ears and is easy to see. Hair growing in ears suggests *wasted energy and a desire not to listen*.

HAIRY EARS

Heavy hair growth in ears accompanied by heavy hair loss on the head suggests talents and energy are being wasted. This may be true as well of one who has Hairy Ears but has little hair on the body.

Hairy Ears suggest an individual may be working too hard at what is not working. For example, one can be working too hard at a relationship that is not working or working too hard making money in a job that is problematic or a job not making use of one's talents or gifts. Hairy Ears also can reveal a stubborn, opinionated individual who doesn't want to listen.

Often, Hairy Ears indicate that one is getting old. An old Hairy Ears Individual may not have made the best use of his or her gifts or talents. However, *it is never too late.*

If a Hairy Ears Individual learns what Hairy Ears reveal, he may be awakened to changes he might want to make.

THE HAIRLINE

The hairline frames the upper part of the face. It forms in adolescence and provides information about this period in a person's life. Hairlines reveal socialization skills and give clues as to where one might succeed in business. The hairline corresponds to the Water element.

Shape shows interest in ideas, others, or business

Basic hairline shapes are curved, squared, expansive, M-Shaped and Widow's Peak. Hairline shape tells *where one's interest lies.*

CURVED HAIRLINE

A rounded hairline is a Curved Hairline. A Curved Hairline reveals interest in others. It suggests a polite, considerate individual with good socialization skills and possibly a strict upbringing. People with Curved Hairlines tend to place high value on family and friends.

Curved Hairline Individuals like to be around others and do well in people-centered careers. A sentimental nature is suggested, and when it comes to clearing clutter, they may have trouble getting rid of gifts. Over-concern about the opinions of others can be one of their challenges.

A Curved Hairline partner might have a history of being well-behaved, but there is a saying that the well-behaved rarely make history. Curved Hairline Individuals often have more interest in relationships than

FACE READING FOR LOVE

Curved Hairline

Square Hairline

Expansive Hairline

M-shaped Hairline

WIDOW'S pEAk

making it big in headlines or business. However, when it comes to business, a Curved Hairline suggests a considerate individual with a good work ethic.

If you have a Curved Hairline, are dating, and are more interested in family than career, politely make this known. With a Curved Hairline, you tend to place others' interests before your own.

SQUARE HAIRLINE

A hairline horizontal on top and vertical on the sides is a Square Hairline. This hairline reveals interest in business. The more angular the shape, the more career-oriented an individual is likely to be. Square Hairlines are most often found on men.

When a Square Hairline is *wide* it suggests an unrestricted approach to life. Commonly, those with this hairline experienced a freer childhood or were rebellious growing up. They make their own rules. Executives and business leaders are often seen with *wide*, Square Hairlines.

Square Hairlines of *medium width* suggest natural team players. They may question rules but work well with others. Their interest is balanced between work and home life; they tend to be loyal to both employer and family. A *medium width* Square Hairline brings a gift for working in harmony.

EXPANSIVE HAIRLINE

A hairline that recedes at the corners is an Expansive Hairline. It reveals an expansive mind. This hairline tells of a keen interest in finding new ways to do things. Expansive Hairline Individuals have a gift for coming up with ideas beyond what is logical to most others' minds.

An Expansive Hairline on a *high and wide forehead* tells of a pioneering nature and one who creates opportunities. This hairline brings success in work that requires travel overseas. When it comes to doing business, this person prefers a fast pace.

An Expansive Hairline on a *high and narrow forehead* reveals a different pace and focus. Working as a scientist or philosopher are examples of areas in which this individual might succeed.

A partner with an Expansive Hairline will reach beyond that which is known to find answers. Such partners are likely to take intuitive leaps in thinking and jump to conclusions.

WIDOW'S PEAK

A hairline that points down in the center is a Widow's Peak Hairline. A peak is considered a universal attractor and suggests an interest in seduction, even though individuals with a Widow's Peak might not dress or act seductively. Their gift of magnetism can be used to their advantage in both business and relationships. Because of a strong desire to be admired, they may feel unsettled at times. Men don't often have this hairline, but when they do, it suggests a gentle, sensitive nature.

The Widow's Peak is so named because widows with this hairline were found not to stay widows very long. A Widow's Peak hairline is said to attract boyfriends easily (or girlfriends as the case may be) and relationships in general.

M-SHAPED HAIRLINE

The masculine version of the Widow's Peak is the M-Shaped Hairline. It is a hairline in the shape of an "M" and is seen primarily on men. It reveals charisma, interest in leadership, and artistic tendencies. Politicians benefit from having this hairline as do creative types and lovers.

An M-Shaped Hairline date might magnetize you with his (or her) charm. You may be swayed; know your boundaries.

Hairlines wide don't hide

Most hairlines are the width of the forehead. However, hairlines can be wider or narrower than the forehead's width. A hairline's width reveals *freedom or inhibition*.

High Hairline

Low Hairline

Wide Hairline

Narrow Hairline

WIDE HAIRLINE

A hairline wider than the forehead is a Wide Hairline. It suggests a feeling of freedom and reveals independent-minded individuals. These individuals desire to expand experiences and are gifted for work in which they are in charge.

Wide Hairlines suggest a rebellious spirit. Wide Hairline Individuals tend not to be overly concerned with others' opinions and often find it challenging following others' directions.

If your Wide Hairline partner has a monotonous job, with rigid rules, in a confined working space, he or she might be very frustrated and want to quit. Wide Hairline Individuals often cherish a sense of freedom more than money. Money might not be your partner's priority, but when an individual's heart is in his or her work he or she is likely to make more money.

NARROW HAIRLINE

A hairline narrower than the forehead is a Narrow Hairline. It suggests inhibition that began in adolescence. Hair growing close to the eyes reveals the individual feels a need for protection.

Narrow Hairline Individuals are inclined to play by the rules. As a result, they work well with others. They tend to be considerate. Some find it challenging when it comes to standing up for themselves. This is more likely when wispy hairs are found along a hairline's vertical edge. Wispy hairs found here reveal an individual who hides feelings when hurt.

If you have wispy hairs, you may cover up your feelings due to fear and may hold back in saying what you should. By standing up for yourself, you can reduce the likelihood of attracting individuals who desire to take advantage of you.

Low hairlines last longer

A hairline might be high or low on the forehead. Hairlines are likely to rise over time. Hairline height reveals early *rebellion or repression*.

HIGH HAIRLINE

When a hairline looks high or appears to be slightly receding, it is a High Hairline. On a relatively young individual this can tell of rebellious teen years. However, when a hairline rises in midlife, it reveals more of the head along with the gifts of drive and ambition.

A High Hairline partner is likely to be highly motivated and have a high opinion of his- or herself.

LOW HAIRLINE

When the horizontal aspect of a hairline is closer to the eyebrows than average, it is a Low Hairline. It suggests possible repression when growing up and can reveal early life was difficult. Parents may not have let such an individual be his- or herself or may have had trouble accepting their child's individuality. For individuals who overcome limitations of early years, a Low Hairline shows the gift of inner strength.

If balding from front to back, a Low Hairline Individual takes longer to go bald. Because of this, Low Hairline Individuals may look young longer than those with High Hairlines. A Low Hairline can be a gift when the hairline begins to move.

A rough edge suggests a rough beginning

To determine hairline smoothness, examine the way the hairs line up. Focus on the hairline's edge, not the shape. The hairline's smoothness tells of *life in teen years* and *socialization skills*.

EVEN HAIRLINE

When the edge is even, it is an Even Hairline. It suggests a non-traumatic adolescence, but this is not always the case. Some with this hairline grew up in difficult or chaotic households but were able to detach and not internalize the negative effects. Others had a rough home life but supportive friends to whom they could turn. An Even Hairline brings the gift of good socialization skills.

Some hairlines are extremely even. An *extremely* Even Hairline can tell of a strict upbringing or repression during the teen years. Extremely Even Hairline Individuals may be somewhat inhibited or lack a true sense of self. Breaking free from the influence of a very controlled upbringing can be their challenge. Those who have worked through this challenge, and now have a true sense of self, have received a true gift.

JAGGED HAIRLINE

When hairs at a hairline's border zig in and zag out, the hairline appears rough and is a Jagged Hairline. It reveals a rough time in teen years and can tell of early life trauma. It shows negative effects were deeply felt. A gift of this hairline is the inner strength to have gotten through this difficult period.

When a Jagged Hairline is *low* on a forehead, the consequences of difficult early years are more likely to be carried though life. When *high*, the past tends to have less influence on the present.

A partner with a Jagged Hairline may have gone through teen years that were not easy. This can bring the gift of compassion for others who are not having an easy time. But some individuals with a Jagged Hairline make life rough for others due to their own difficult start. A partner who experienced trauma will benefit from a smooth, stable, supportive relationship.

THE FOREHEAD

The forehead shows thinking style as well as basic character and creativity. The forehead gives clues to intellectual focus and suggests gifts and challenges regarding career. The need to use inherited talents is told at the top.

The more a person's hair covers his or her forehead, the more a person will want to keep some things private. The more exposed, the more likely a person will talk about anything. The forehead corresponds to the Water element.

The top tells of inherited talents

The forehead extends from hairline to eyebrows. On a balding individual, the forehead starts where the hairline was before it started to move. The upper portion of a forehead may be straight or rounded. The upper forehead tells if *ancestral talents need to be used.*

ROUNDED UPPER FOREHEAD

When the uppermost part of a forehead is rounded, it is a Rounded Upper Forehead. A Rounded Upper Forehead reveals important ancestral gifts and talents need to be used. It does not reveal, however, what the gifts are. Roundness at the top also indicates creativity, imagination, intuition, and one who may have a keen interest in spirituality.

Your partner may have a gift, such as musical talent, passed down from hardworking ancestors unable to put the gift to good use.

STRAIGHT UPPER FOREHEAD

When the uppermost part of a forehead is *not rounded*, it is a Straight Upper Forehead. Straight Upper Foreheads reveal those who need to make their own way in the world. A Straight Upper Forehead Individual often has talents unlike those of his or her ancestors.

A Straight Upper Forehead Individual may have abilities that puzzle the parents. They can't figure out from whom he or she inherited the gifts. Talents are different than those of the family.

Learning style is learned from the slant; creativity is seen in the curve

When viewing a face from profile, a forehead may appear straight, slanted, or curved. Many people have a forehead that is a blending of different types. To determine the forehead's shape, look at the face from the side. Forehead shape shows *style of thinking*.

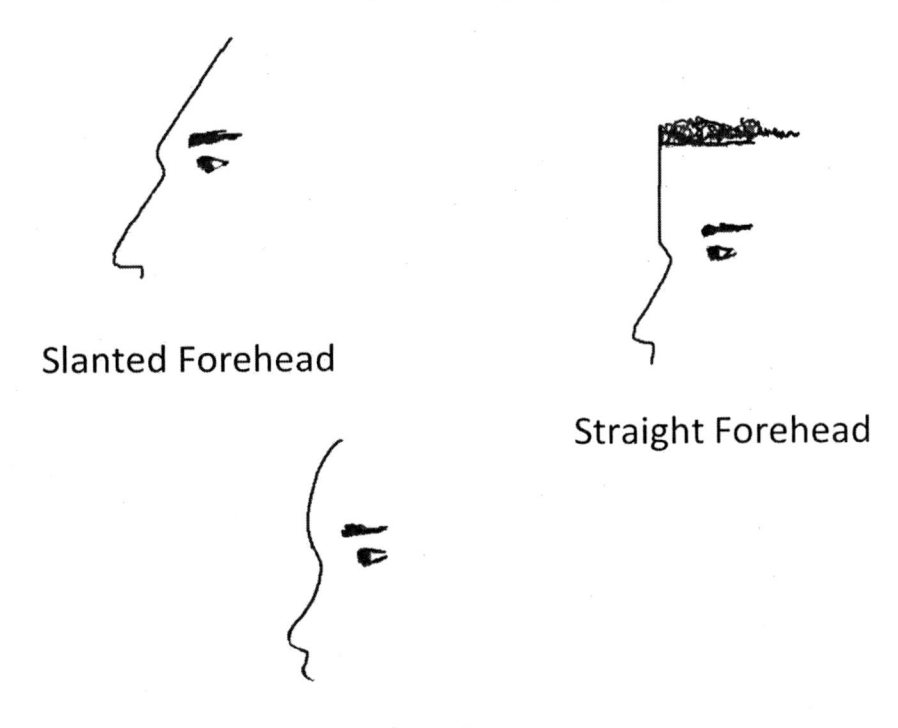

Slanted Forehead

Straight Forehead

Round Forehead

SLANTED FOREHEAD

A forehead that angles back is a Slanted Forehead. A Slanted Forehead suggests a speedy style of thinking. This forehead shape may be thought of as a "backward focused forehead" as it tells of easy access to stored data and memory.

Slanted Forehead Individuals have a talent for quickly recalling facts, and when it comes to making decisions are able to make them fast. They have a preference for proven procedures and following them helps speed their thought processes. They have a gift for learning quickly but the challenge of restlessness. These individuals don't like wasting time.

A Slanted Forehead suggests a rapid responder. In business, a Slanted Forehead is useful in situations in which thinking is required on the spot; in sales, for example, having this forehead shape is helpful in making deals. A Slanted Forehead benefits actors as it accelerates learning and recalling scripted lines. In sports that require automatic reactions, it provides an advantage; an advantage *enhanced when the chin slants in.*

When talking with your Slanted Forehead partner, you may find it best to leave out unnecessary information and get right to the point. Speed up the pace as well. If you speak too slowly, he or she may jump ahead to conclusions or jump up and down indicating impatience with you.

When dating, if a Slanted Forehead Individual tells you he or she needs time to think things over before becoming more involved, you may wish to give thought to what is revealed. Those with this forehead are known to be fast decision makers. Perhaps your date is just being polite. *But*, if your date's forehead is *very tall*, this could indicate he or she might truly need more time to think before making a decision.

STRAIGHT FOREHEAD

A vertical forehead is a Straight Forehead. This forehead shape reveals an individual who learns best when information is presented in a straightforward way. A Straight Forehead tells of a linear style of thinking. Those with this forehead tend to be strong minded, determined, and stubborn. They like to work on their own.

For a Straight Forehead Individual to learn something, he or she needs to understand it firmly. Information presented should be logical and clear. Instructions are best received when given step-by-step. Straight Forehead Individuals can take longer to learn something, but what is learned usually sticks. The Straight Forehead brings a gift in situations that require a solid grasp of a subject and not just quick recall of facts. When those with this forehead learn *how* they learn, they are able to retain *what* they learn practically forever.

A Straight Forehead may be thought of as a "present-focused forehead"; to learn something, these individuals need to stay present and focused. They do not learn well under pressure or when information is presented hastily, out of sequence, or in a random way. When overwhelmed, a Straight Forehead Individual's mind shuts down to learning anything further.

If teaching something to your Straight Forehead partner, it is best to use a clear, orderly approach. What seems logical to you may not be logical to your partner. When you see a blank look, your partner is lost. Back up, slow down, and explain again.

When in a conversation with a Slanted Forehead Individual, you might find that a response to what you said is sometimes given long afterward.

ROUND FOREHEAD

When a forehead is curved when viewed from profile, it is a Round Forehead. Round Foreheads may be thought of as "forward thinking foreheads"; they reveal original thinking and imaginative minds. Round Forehead Individuals' thinking expands beyond what is known in the present; their minds are not limited to information from three-dimensional planes. A Round Forehead reveals a creative style of thinking.

Round Foreheads show imagination and an adventurous spirit. These individuals do best in a loosely structured environment and don't do as well when restricted by rigid systems and rules. To access their gift for devising unique solutions and innovative ideas, they should not feel limited. Some individuals with Round Foreheads might appear to be in a dreamy state at times, but are likely alert and receptive to inspiration, which often comes in a flash.

Their gift of creativity might also bring the gift of a long life. Creative individuals often don't aspire to retire, as the stimulation of imagination gives their work purpose and drives them. Many Round Forehead Individuals create their own work and don't have a job from which they are forced to retire.

A mind cluttered with facts and figures may be unable to catch what is seeking to be revealed. Round Forehead Individuals have an easier time turning within. This can bring forth great works. Inventors, writers, artists, composers, and mystics may benefit from having some roundness to their forehead. Visionary leaders benefit from an imaginative mind as well.

You may have a Round Forehead and may answer questions in a roundabout way. A date with a *Slanted* Forehead might desire a quicker pace, may have trouble following your train of thought, and might tell you that you are avoiding questions.

Span of interests is shown in the width

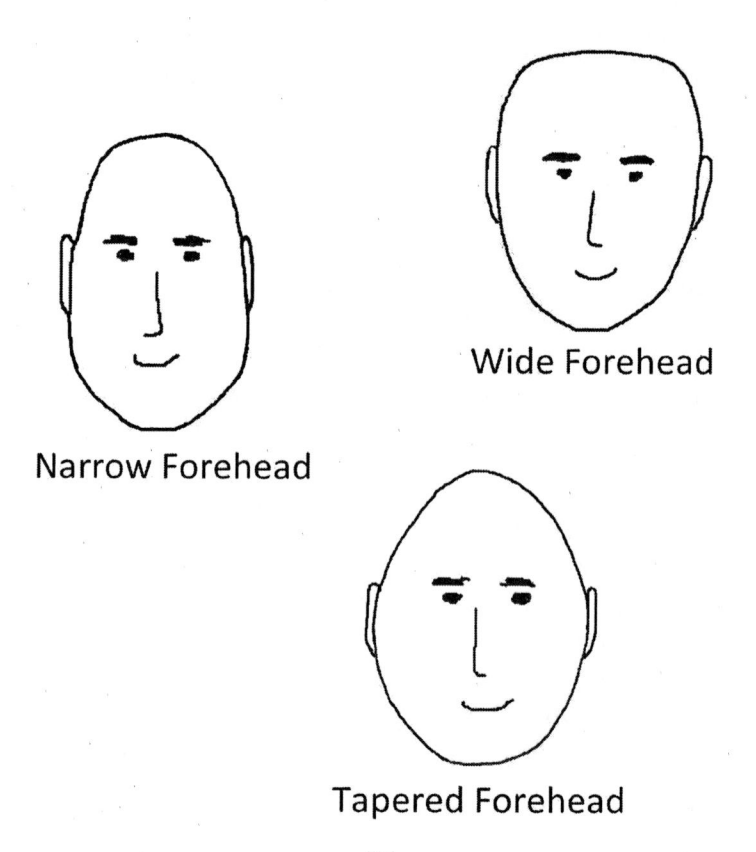

Narrow Forehead

Wide Forehead

Tapered Forehead

Wide Foreheads are found on broad faces, as well as faces wide only at the top. Narrow Foreheads are found on narrow faces, as well as those wide only at the bottom. If a forehead looks to be wide or narrow, it likely is. Forehead width shows *range of interests or knowledge*.

WIDE FOREHEAD

When a forehead appears wider than average above the ears it is a Wide Forehead. Wide Foreheads suggest a broad range of interests and knowledge. The focus of these individuals' minds tends not to be limited.

Wide Forehead Individuals seek new situations and challenges, have leadership ability, and can excel as entrepreneurs. When a Wide Forehead is *broadest at the top*, this tells of increased analytical abilities. When the *top bulges*, this suggests an individual who is driven.

A Wide Forehead that is also *tall* reveals a person who sets his or her sights high. This forehead shows a gift for making money when doing business overseas. A Wide Forehead that is *short* reveals intelligence for practical purposes; these individuals excel when using their hands or their wit.

A Wide Forehead Individual will not be happy in a job in which his or her talents are confined to a narrow range. This forehead tells of a dislike of details and a potential challenge staying focused.

A partner with a *short* Wide Forehead may be down to earth, but may have a need to be looked up to. A partner with a *tall* Wide Forehead may often be up in a plane, expanding business opportunities. When not literally among the clouds, his or her mind may be.

NARROW FOREHEAD

When a forehead appears narrower than average above the ears, it is a Narrow Forehead. Narrow Foreheads suggest a narrow range of interests and focus. These individuals are often experts in specialized fields. A Narrow Forehead brings the challenge of a restricted point of view, but also bestows gifts of dedication to purpose and a deep understanding of details.

Your Narrow Forehead partner may be a creature of habit and set in his or her ways. If you have a *Wide* Forehead and a broader perspective, you may be able to view this as the gift of persistence.

When dating an individual with a *tall* Narrow Forehead, you may find him or her to be exceptionally knowledgeable on an obscure subject and highly respected for his or her intelligence. Delving deeply into the details of a specific area of expertise, you date's interest knows no limits. In common social situations or when attending a party that has no specific purpose, he or she might have limited interest and little to say.

TAPERED FOREHEAD

A forehead that narrows at the top is a Tapered Forehead. This forehead suggests enthusiasm and an adventurous spirit. Individuals with this forehead excel in careers requiring a rapid pace, but don't do well performing monotonous tasks or working in a small, enclosed space. A Tapered Forehead tells of an individual who desires to speed things up and has a gift for it.

When a Tapered Forehead is *tall*, this reveals intellectual intelligence and individuals who passionately make a point of using their mind. Scholars and cerebral individuals excited about their work often have *tall* Tapered Foreheads.

When a Tapered Forehead is *short*, it reveals one who finds it challenging to be still. These individuals don't do well thinking for extended periods of time. A *short* Tapered Forehead suggests physical gifts and one eager to put them to use. Movement is important; therefore, impulsiveness can be their challenge.

Short suggests a down to earth focus

To determine forehead height, when reading your own face, you can use your hand as a measuring device. Place your fingers horizontally across your forehead. If the forehead is five fingers it is a Tall Forehead. Four fingers or less is a Short Forehead. If reading the face of another (who knows you are doing a face reading), measure using his or her hand.

An alternative way is to look at the face. When the longest part of the face is the forehead, it is a Tall Forehead. When the shortest part of the face is the forehead, it is a Short Forehead. Forehead height reveals a *mental or physical focus*.

Tall Forehead

Short Forehead

TALL FOREHEAD

A Tall Forehead reveals a mental focus and a person intellectually inclined. Tall Forehead Individuals give high priority to education, because this forehead brings a gift for using the mind. When a forehead is *very* tall, however, it indicates a person might spend too much time inside his or her head. Tall Forehead Individuals need to think things through.

Tall Foreheads Individuals set their sights high. In business, a *wide* Tall Forehead suggests one who can excel as an executive in a large corporation or one who might succeed in politics. When a *wide* Tall Forehead has a hairline with upper corners that recede, this shows success may be found doing business overseas. Those with a *narrow* Tall Forehead find more success behind a desk. Their expertise is in their narrower range of focus; working with numbers, or in research or science, might be where they succeed.

If your partner has a Tall Forehead, he or she may spend money on intellectual development such as attending seminars, taking classes, and earning educational degrees. Your partner is likely to view this as a wise investment. You may or may not see it the same way.

Wealth may be found moving around for those whose hairlines recede in the *corners* of a *wide* Tall Forehead. If this is your partner, he or she has the potential to make big money in work involving international travel. But, with so much moving around, your partner won't be able to spend as much time around you.

SHORT FOREHEAD

A Short Forehead suggests a physical focus and a person who learns by doing. Short Forehead Individuals learn from experience and from taking a hands-on approach. They have an easier time generating *new* ideas when they don't overload their mind with *old* knowledge gathered from books.

Short Foreheads tell of intelligence that is instinctual or intuitive. Gut feelings play a big part in the decisions these individuals make.

Short Forehead Individuals function best when they don't overanalyze. Most find it challenging to be stuck behind a desk. Tending to be nonconformists, many are most successful working for themselves. These individuals are often physically gifted and excel using their body or hands. They are also opinionated, and if they encounter something with which they don't agree, they say so, often in a bold and daring way.

You may have a partner with a Short Forehead who is naturally more physical than intellectual. Time spent in bed with you when not sleeping may not be spent reading books. You may view this as a gift…or a challenge.

THE EYEBROWS

Eyebrows are one of the more important facial features. They provide powerful visual clues to personality; they reveal drive, passion, and vitality. Eyebrows show focus, thought patterns, clarity of character, areas for achievement, and visionary potential. Life outlook and desire for friendships are suggested, as well as how quickly a person wants to get close.

The right and left brow are oftentimes different. The right side shows the public or business side, whereas the left side shows the private or personal side. When eyebrows don't match, read both eyebrows.

A single vertical groove between the eyebrows suggests focused thinking as well as greater potential for an explosive temper. Four lines seen between the eyebrows reveal an inquiring mind and a person better at handling anger.

Eyebrows take their shape naturally from the underlying bone structure, but many people tweeze or wax them into a different shape. Some shave them off and draw them in. A "shape change" reveals how a person wishes to be seen. For an eyebrow to reveal an individual's natural nature, the hair needs to grow in its natural form. Eyebrows correspond to the Wood element.

Approach to life and thinking shows in the shape

The basic eyebrow shapes are Straight, Curved, and Angled. Eyebrow shape reveals *approach to life and thinking*.

Straight Eyebrows

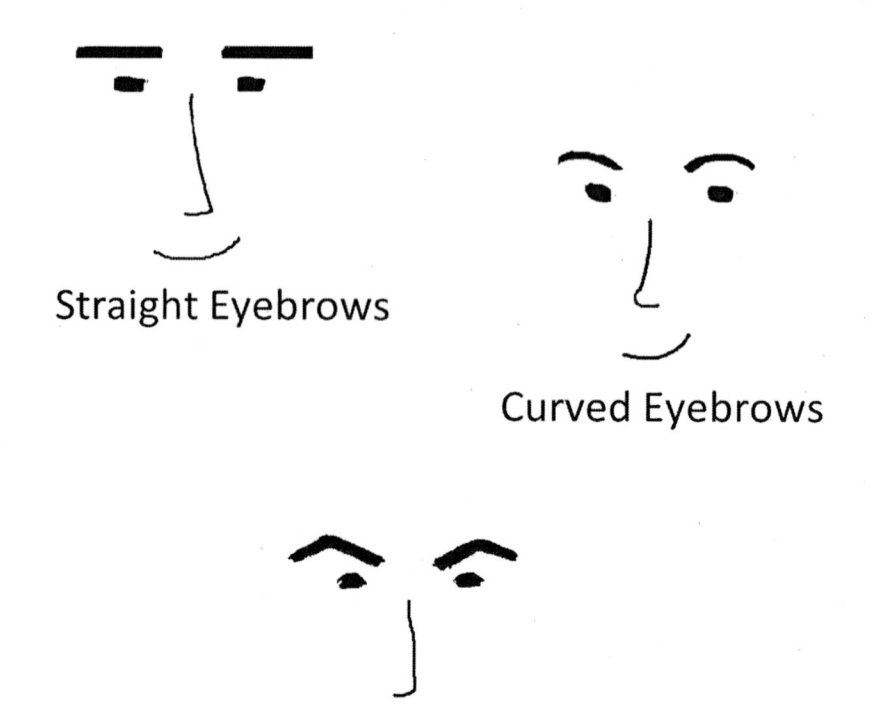

Curved Eyebrows

Angled Eyebrows

STRAIGHT EYEBROWS

Straight Eyebrows are in the shape of a straight line and reveal a straightforward approach. They suggest sound judgment and emotional detachment when making decisions. Before accepting something as true, Straight Eyebrows Individuals want facts.

Straight Eyebrows suggest logical, practical individuals who stay on course without letting emotions interfere. They excel at organizing and straightening things out. When it comes to business, their focus is often more on analysis, efficiency, and accomplishing than on developing human relationships. Managers, technicians, and scientists have an advantage with naturally Straight Eyebrows.

Eyebrows that are straight due to an eyebrow "shape change" can reveal an individual who is not as logical as he or she appears. However, cleaning up eyebrows by removing stray hairs can bring order to one's thoughts.

Those with Straight Eyebrows often choose a life partner based on what is practical and realistic. They make decisions using their head.

If you have a partner with Straight Eyebrows, he or she is likely to think in a straightforward way, taking one topic and following it through to the end. If your brows are not straight, your thoughts don't naturally follow a straight line of thinking. When discussing a topic you may bring up other topics and your partner might ask, "Why are you telling me this?" Your mind may be wired to interconnect, but a Straight Eyebrows partner might have difficulty seeing the connection.

CURVED EYEBROWS

Curved Eyebrows take the form of a curved line and reveal a people approach to thinking. They suggest one concerned about others and receptive to all types of people. Curved Eyebrows project a welcoming look.

Curved Eyebrows Individuals' thoughts are driven by emotions; they learn much from people and life. They have a gift for working with others and for coordinating projects, parties, and events. Curved Eyebrows Individuals can excel in people-focused careers such as real estate, sales, hospitality, healthcare, and entertainment.

Curved Eyebrows Individuals can be very good at making a profit, but are often not focused on career, viewing family or relationships as more important.

When eyebrows are shaved off and exaggerated curved ones drawn in, this communicates a strong desire to please; a desire that may not always be real.

Curved Eyebrows Individuals may have an easier time creating harmony in relationships. It is their nature to be sensitive to the feelings of others and think of others first.

ANGLED EYEBROWS

An Angled Eyebrow contains an apex where the brow changes direction. This direction change occurs in the middle or near the end. Often these eyebrows are in the shape of a wide, inverted "V." Angled Eyebrows reveal an ambitious approach to thinking and a need to be in control.

Angled Eyebrows Individuals have strong personalities that can intimidate others; they want their way, which can be difficult on others. They are not those who follow others. *Extra hair found at the apex* suggests an individual who gets energized by conflict or by being in the midst of working on a long project. *When the outer end is higher*, this reveals a dramatic individual.

Angled Eyebrows tell of a need to take action. These individuals have a gift for leadership and a nature that loves to manage and direct. Some have difficulty delegating work, feeling they can do a better job themselves. In youth, Angled Eyebrows Individuals tend to be interested in material things; with age, their thoughts often turn to spiritual matters.

Angled Eyebrows Individuals cut through obstacles and create opportunities. Success is often found through creativity. Angled Eyebrows can be beneficial for business, innovation, and leading others but may bring challenges when it comes to personal relationships.

Angled Eyebrows Individuals have an adventurous spirit that is not easily satisfied. Most gamblers of one form or another have a variation of Angled Eyebrows. Weak individuals are often attracted to Angled Eyebrows Individuals, but Angled Eyebrows Individuals do not find weakness attractive.

An Angled Eyebrows Individual may give you driving directions and tell you where to park. If so, consider the tone, for he or she may only be trying to help. Angled Eyebrows Individuals have a natural need to feel in control of *situations*; however, a helpful car mate may have no interest in controlling *you*.

Your Angled Eyebrow partner sees things his or her way and may have some difficulty seeing things your way.

Slant projects presence

Most eyebrows grow in a horizontal direction. But some slant up and some slant down. Eyebrow slant reveals level of *self-assurance*.

UPWARD SLANTING EYEBROWS

When an eyebrow begins low and rises high it is an Upward Slanting Eyebrow. Upward Slanting Eyebrows present a powerful presence and reveal a strong drive. These individuals go for want they want with determination.

Upward Slanting Eyebrows suggest a high level of self-assurance. These individuals don't look as if they need any help. Most often they don't, but this is not always the case. However, their intimidating appearance hinders others from offering assistance. Upward Slanting Eyebrows reveal one who can be domineering, and these brows warn others to be careful with what they do or say. Upward Slanting Eyebrows have the potential to keep people away.

Upward Slanting Eyebrows Individuals thrive on thrills and get frustrated when things move too slowly or become boring or tedious. Both work and love life needs to be interesting.

If you have just started dating an Upward Slanting Eyebrows Individual, you may be aware of his or her drive, determination, and self-assurance. Concern for building a relationship slowly may not be his or her focus. That does not mean that *you* are not the focus. Those with these eyebrows go after what they want and tend to move fast.

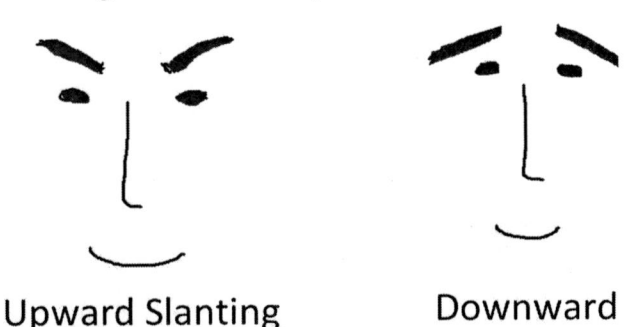

Upward Slanting Eyebrows   **Downward Slanting Eyebrows**

DOWNWARD SLANTING EYEBROWS

When an eyebrow begins high and is lower at the end, it is a Downward Slanting Eyebrow. Downward Slanting Eyebrows Individuals look as if they need help. Their strength can be their perceived weakness. Helpful people see a person with these eyebrows and ask if they can help. Easy access to assistance is a gift of these brows.

Downward Slanting Eyebrows suggest a lower level of self-assurance than found in those with straight or up slanting brows. Knowing others will be there when needed can bring peace of mind to those with this worried look. But those who rely too much on others don't learn to handle situations themselves.

Most Downward Slanting Eyebrows Individuals do not desire to be leaders. Many with good ideas excel behind the scenes working in positions such as advisors, strategists, or copywriters for announcers on television. And, the gift of easy access to support might give a Downward Slanting Eyebrows Individual an advantage when it comes to obtaining contributions for causes, candidates, or organizations.

Your Downward Slanting Eyebrows partner may look as if he or she could use some help, which you may be willing and able to provide. Many with Downward Slanting Eyebrows are gracious and grateful, but some whine, complain, and are never satisfied. If you are feeling used too much, you may decide not to help as much, which may turn out to help even more. Your partner might learn self-reliance.

You might find your date with Downward Slanting Eyebrows to be a very seductive individual.

Passion is revealed in the thickness

Eyebrows vary in thickness. If an eyebrow looks thick or thin, it likely is. When brow make-up is worn, closer observation is required to determine brow thickness. Eyebrow thickness reveals *the amount of vitality and passion*.

THICK EYEBROWS

When eyebrow hairs are abundant, eyebrows are Thick Eyebrows. Thick Eyebrows indicate a good amount of vitality and passion. They bring a gift for handling multiple thoughts and things at one time; emotionally, these individuals have the ability to deal with many people. The thicker the eyebrows, the more assertive an individual is likely to be. *Dark* colored Thick Eyebrows suggest extra vitality.

Thick Eyebrows reveal action-oriented thinkers who need to put their thoughts to good use. These brows indicate a strong drive. Thick Eyebrows Individuals want to be in charge and become frustrated when things move slowly or don't go their way. They have a potential for angry outbursts. They sometimes complicate simple matters.

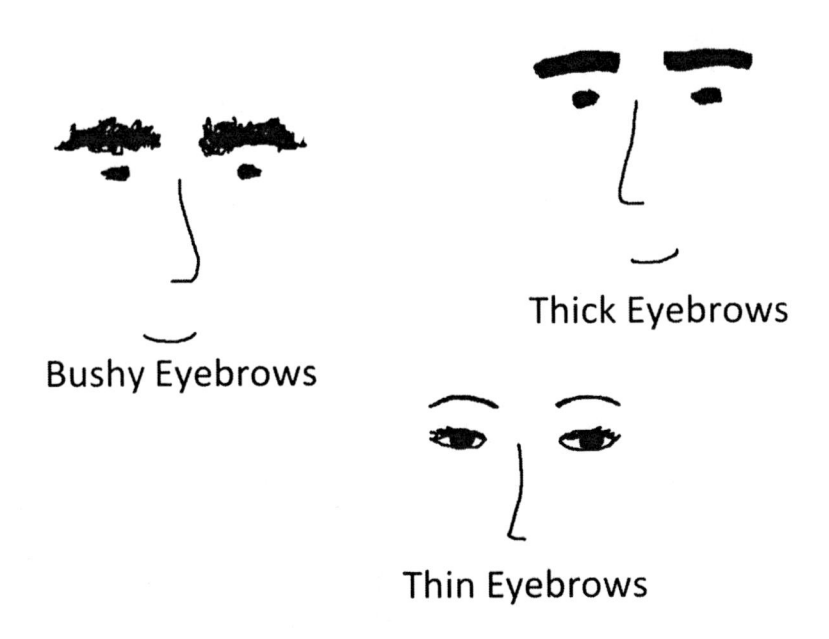

Bushy Eyebrows

Thick Eyebrows

Thin Eyebrows

Thick Eyebrows Individuals may divide their time between family, friends, and business associates with energy to spare. Thick Eyebrows suggest one with *energy* to handle more than one sexual or romantic relationship simultaneously. Having the *time*, or getting away with it, is another matter.

Thick Eyebrows suggest a powerful liver and the ability to process toxic substances more easily than most. A Thick Eyebrows Individual often can handle more alcohol and drugs before suffering physical damage. Some with Thick Eyebrows are drawn to chemicals to manage their emotions and calm their active mind.

Very Thick Eyebrows are usually seen only on males. If dating a woman with *very* Thick Eyebrows, you may find she has a fighting spirit. Energy may increase during lively discussions. Arguments will tend to energize her. These brows reveal passion, which may be put to good use in business, sports, and sex.

BUSHY EYEBROWS

Bushy Eyebrows are Thick Eyebrows that reveal similar traits, but do so to a greater extent. The hairs of Bushy Eyebrows are profuse and unruly. Bushy Eyebrows suggest an overflow of vitality and passion. Enthusiastic about their beliefs, these are spirited individuals who have strong potential for a domineering temperament.

Your Bushy Eyebrows date may be passionately trying to make a point, but you might perceive him or her to be argumentative.

THIN EYEBROWS

Slender eyebrows are Thin Eyebrows. They suggest limited energy when dealing with people, thoughts, or things. Discipline, order, and sensitivity are revealed. Thin Eyebrows tell of refined passion and drive.

Thin Eyebrows don't intimidate others, which allows for easy access to help. Arguments typically tire Thin Eyebrows Individuals; they try to avoid them. Thin Eyebrows with *soft hairs* suggest a flexible and adaptable individual who prefers everyone get along.

Thin Eyebrows Individuals do best organizing and executing their life around priorities and are less effective in multitasking, in cluttered surroundings, or around too many people. They can easily become irritated if interrupted when concentrating on something. When their thoughts are focused and clear, they have the ability to see things others might miss.

Thin Eyebrows Individuals need to practice economy of energy and when dating may find it less taxing focusing on one person at a time. Thin Eyebrows Individuals are sensitive to others, which is a blessing to those others. But, some are too concerned with opinions of others and therefore may be hurt easily.

You may want your Thin Eyebrows partner to do several things simultaneously. He or she is less effective this way. Arguing about it might leave your partner too exhausted to get anything done.

These eyebrows reveal a gift for dealing with fine points and small details, which could mean your Thin Eyebrows partner is neat and tidy around the house. This can mean less work for you!

Time to act is told in the distance

All eyebrows are not spaced the same distance. Some lie low to the eyes and some high above. Eyebrow height is the eye-to-brow distance. Eyebrow height reveals *time between thinking and acting.*

HIGH EYEBROWS

Eyebrows high above the eyes are High Eyebrows. They reveal cautious thinking; before acting these individuals take a good amount of time.

When initially meeting others, High Eyebrows Individuals might seem cold, but they size things up before opening up; High Eyebrows Individuals need to feel safe and comfortable first. And, concerning comfort, High Eyebrows Individuals often find comfort in certain dates, special numbers, ceremonies, and rituals. Most are sensible, but some can be somewhat superstitious.

High Eyebrows Individuals are selective about friends, purchases, and decisions and give careful thought to these matters. Friends benefit

High Eyebrows   **Low Eyebrows**

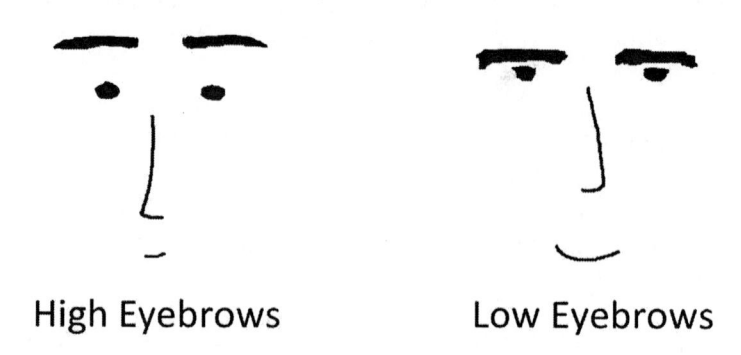

from a High Eyebrows Individual's ability to hold back, as secrets are kept more easily. Businesses benefit too. But some people are turned off by their wary approach; it is not always understood.

In a situation in which immediate help is needed, such as an accident scene, a High Eyebrows Individual might pause before getting involved. A decision to turn away may have nothing to do with lack of caring or concern. A High Eyebrows Individual is likely to consider the legal consequences of jumping in and helping out; or may think, "It is his or her karma" and decide it is best not to interfere.

If on a first date you notice your date has High Eyebrows, it is wise not to move too close too fast. Be mindful of his or her personal space. Let your date initiate a hug.

If you have a High Eyebrows partner, feel honored. High Eyebrows Individuals tend to be quite discriminating about those with whom they spend time.

LOW EYEBROWS

Eyebrows close to the eyes are Low Eyebrows. Low Eyebrows reveal a spontaneous approach and down-to-earth nature. It is natural for those with these brows to spend little time thinking before acting or speaking.

Low Eyebrows Individuals are perceived as helpful, friendly, genuine, and sincere. They prefer quick involvement, like giving advice, often like giving hugs, and tend to be frank. At times, Low Eyebrows Individuals speak without thinking or considering all facts; problems can arise when they move too fast.

Low Eyebrows Individuals' ability to physically respond quickly is valuable when immediate action is needed, such as when working in an emergency room or as a firefighter. And, their gift for rapid verbal response provides an advantage in occupations in which thinking and speaking are required on the spot. Sportscasters, salespeople, and workshop presenters needing quick answers to questions benefit from having Low Eyebrows.

Individuals who are single and seeking may benefit from the ability to think and act without hesitating. An individual with Low Eyebrows who sees someone of interest will not hesitate to say something before the interesting person gets away.

An interested Low Eyebrows date may speak quickly as something comes to mind. This shows enthusiasm; a positive sign. Take note, however, that a date with *thick* Low Eyebrows might get carried away in the heat of the moment and make promises that he or she can't keep.

If you are looking for a partner for tennis doubles, an individual with Low Eyebrows acts instantly, providing an advantage. A tennis partner with High Eyebrows will tend to be slower acting, but when losing a match won't be as likely to lose his or her cool on the court.

Space suggests span of interests

The average space between the eyebrows is one-and-one-half to two fingers wide. (This is based on using the hand of the person being read. When reading the face of another individual who does not know that his or her face is being read, you'll need to use your mind to measure the distance.) Eyebrow spacing reveals *concentration of thoughts.*

WIDE SPACED BROWS

Eyebrows spaced more than two finger-widths apart are Wide Spaced Brows. Wide Spaced Brows reveal an open mind and thoughts spread

Narrow Spaced Brows

Wide Spaced Brows

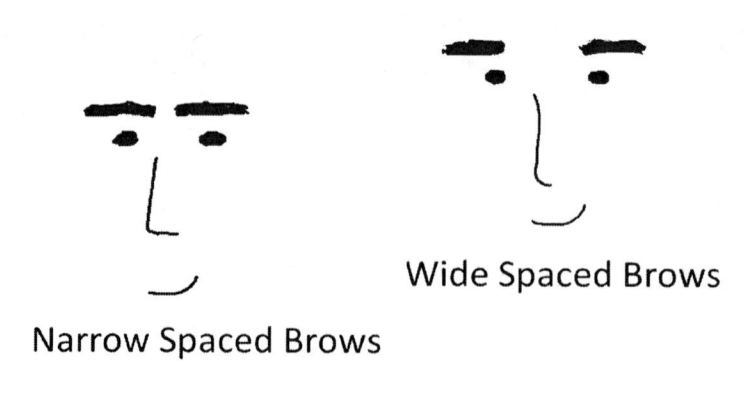

United Brow

over a wide range. Wide Spaced Brows suggest one has many interests. These individuals tend to see the simple pleasures in life easily, but when the space is *very* wide, might be too carefree.

Wide Spaced Brows suggest patience and ease in getting along with a wide variety of people. This is useful when working with diverse types, such as in customer service or sales. They make good team players. Wide Spaced Brows Individuals also make good conversationalists because of their wide span of interests. Their responses might be slower, however, because they consider a wider range of thoughts.

Your partner with Wide Spaced Brows may be blessed with the gift of an optimistic outlook but have the challenge of staying focused.

NARROW SPACED BROWS

Eyebrows one finger-width apart or less are Narrow Spaced Brows. Narrow Spaced Brows suggest a narrow range of interests and centered, focused thoughts.

Narrow Spaced Brows indicate a gift for details, precision, and accuracy. These individuals may find success as accountants and editors; they can excel in legal, research, or technical positions. The speed with which they process thoughts helps get work done quickly. With thoughts concentrated in front of their eyes, however, Narrow Space Brows Individuals can have challenges seeing the big picture.

Narrow Spaced Brows Individuals need to be thoughtful of where they focus their attention. They may have difficulty dealing with various types of personalities. Focusing on others, they can become frustrated if a person moves slowly or doesn't see things their way. They are often better off working for themselves or in situations not heavily supervised. They have a more rebellious than easy-going nature. However, when used constructively a rebellious nature is a gift; it can bring up things that need to be changed.

At work your Narrow Spaced Brows partner could be thought of as being difficult when he or she calls attention to a better way of doing things. But, it is the manner in which your partner presents the information that determines how this suggestion is perceived.

Narrow Spaced Brows Individuals do not like moving slowly; your Narrow Spaced Brows partner might be impatient to succeed.

UNITED BROW

Eyebrows that grow together form a United Brow. A United Brow, often called a unibrow, reveals physical and intellectual strength. This eyebrow with no break in hairs tells of no break in thoughts and the challenge of nonstop thinking. United Brow Individuals tend to be exceptionally vital, passionate individuals.

They might look fierce. *Coarse* brow hairs suggest aggressive tendencies and an individual who is more apt to be domineering. These brows reveal a high level of testosterone and a potential for explosive anger. These traits can be channeled constructively into contact sports or the military.

When United Brow hairs are *soft*, it indicates a gentler nature without forceful tendencies. These individuals think constantly and have difficulty relaxing. They are often harder on themselves than they are on others. Insomnia might be a problem for those with a United Brow.

Coarse haired United Brow Individuals looking for a relationship may find their look frightens others or causes others to look away. Hair removal to create a space might help. There is no guarantee of establishing a relationship, but they are likely to get more friendly smiles and more nights of restful sleep.

Length leads to friendships

Eyebrows come in various lengths. Length tells of *desire and energy for friends*.

LONG EYEBROWS

Eyebrows that grow beyond the eyes' length and down the sides are Long Eyebrows. They suggest desire, energy, and patience for friends. Long Eyebrows Individuals tend to be sentimental and may have difficulty parting with friends. Long Eyebrows indicate a gift for friendships.

Long Eyebrows show a long-fused temper, which helps manage anger and helps keep friends. When Long Eyebrows are *very thick* they reveal a person with even more energy for friends and suggests one who might enjoy showing off to them. Long Eyebrows tell of a humanitarian nature, but those not so evolved might be more judgmental.

Your partner with Long Eyebrows likely has many friends. If you want to keep your partner, understand that nurturing friendships takes time.

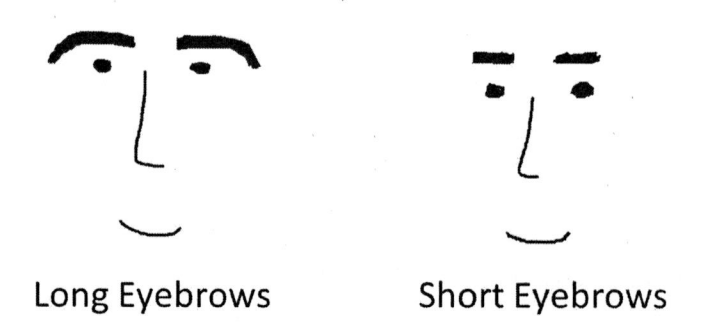

Long Eyebrows   **Short Eyebrows**

SHORT EYEBROWS

An Eyebrow that does not span the eye's entire length is a Short Eyebrow. Physically, Short Eyebrows reveal less vitality than Long Eyebrows. Emotionally, Short Eyebrows suggest independence and self-centered ambition. Mentally, these individuals are motivated by challenges, but when it comes to problems, they often don't want to hear about others' issues. They tend to be somewhat pessimistic. These eyebrows bring a Short Eyebrows Individual a gift for being focused on what is important to him or her.

Short Eyebrows suggest a person without the desire to have a large number of friends or one who does not have the energy for it. Short Eyebrows Individuals know what others give to them they will be expected to give back. They don't desire to take on problems of too many people; they have enough to handle dealing with their own. They can commit to a relationship, but need a sense of freedom. They tend to respond emotionally and may be hurt easily.

Eyebrows can change over time. Eyebrows tend to shorten and thin with age. This shows less energy to put into maintaining lots of friendships as well as less energy when it comes to following through on projects, goals, and plans.

A Short Eyebrows Individual may feel little need to divide time among social obligations. This could bring your Short Eyebrows partner success through work!

Have you just started dating a Short Eyebrows Individual? You may want to know they have a tendency to be blunt.

If you are a friend of a Short Eyebrows Individual, consider yourself a true friend.

Distribution determines the gift

Eyebrow hair distribution is often not the same throughout the brow. More hair may be seen at the beginning, the middle, or the end. (The beginning is next to the nose.) Eyebrow hair distribution reveals at *what stage one best handles projects and thoughts.*

Beginning Brows

Ending Brows

Even Brows

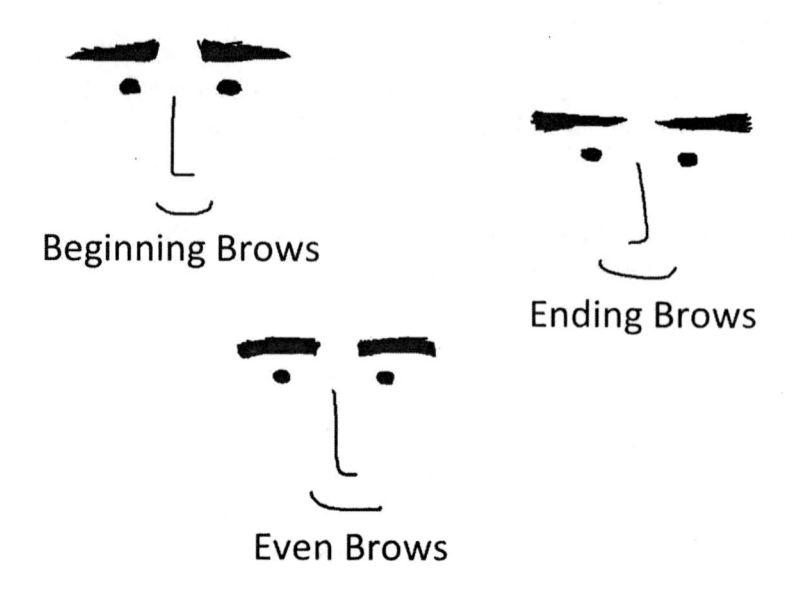

BEGINNING BROWS

When the beginning is the thickest part of the eyebrows, they are Beginning Brows. They reveal a gift for visionary ideas and potential leadership ability. Beginning Brows Individuals' strength is at the start of projects and thoughts. Followers these individuals are not.

Beginning Brows Individuals have a talent for coming up with creative, innovative approaches. They begin with an abundance of thoughts and enthusiasm but often get frustrated with follow through. Dealing with final details can be challenging for them, and when possible is best left to managers, production people, partners, or assistants.

Beginning Brows provide a wealth of ideas, more than may be possible to act on at one time. To help reach goals, Beginning Brows Individuals might want to consider limiting their list to those that are most important.

Your Beginning Brows partner might be good starting projects and tasks around the house but may not always complete them. Unfortunately, there is no way to know for certain at the start if something will get finished.

ENDING BROWS

When the end is the thickest part of an eyebrow, it is an Ending Brow. Ending Brows suggest some slowness in coming up with ideas and starting projects. Ending Brows reveal a person who gains speed and enthusiasm near the end. These individuals are good at organization and with details and have what it takes to get things completed.

Ending Brows Individuals have a gift for taking over tasks and projects and finishing things. They work in a methodical way, take pride in their work, and often have perfectionist tendencies. Ending Brows Individuals can find success in "ending job" positions, for example, working as assistants, managers, or in post-production. They are good at handling the paperwork to finalize agreements.

When planning a trip, an Ending Brows partner can excel in handling details. Turn them over to him or her.

When the beginnings of Ending Brows are much thinner and in a pointed shape, this suggests family might likely receive more attention than career.

EVEN BROWS

When hair thickness is the same throughout the eyebrows, they are Even Brows. Even Brows suggest an even flow of thoughts. Those with these brows take a moderate amount of time to come up with an idea, develop it, and see it through to completion at a moderate pace. When it comes to handling projects or thoughts, enthusiasm and commitment remain steady from start to finish. Even Brows Individuals are good with details and can easily see the complete picture.

An Even Brows partner might get frustrated if you have trouble starting something or trouble completing it. But if you also have Even Brows, this might not be an issue.

Scattered Hairs

Stick-Up, Start-Up Hairs

Long Wild Hairs

SCATTERED HAIRS

When eyebrows are full at the beginning and hairs scatter starting in the middle, they are Scattered Hairs. Scattered Hairs tell of the gift of an active mind but also many unrelated thoughts. This individual is likely to have many projects, goals, or plans going at once.

Hairs scattering from the middle to the end shows that thoughts are stronger at inception. Thinking then expands into different areas, scattering thought power and hampering one's ability to follow through. If hairs are *light and thin*, or if the eyebrow is sparse overall, this suggests less energy and a person who might want to narrow his or her to-do list. When eyebrow hairs are *dark and thick*, and Scattered Hairs not very far apart, this indicates enough energy to get everything done, but focusing is still likely a challenge.

Scattered Hairs indicate a wide range of interests, ideas, and thoughts. A partner with Scattered Hairs is probably not a boring person. These eyebrows, however, can look messy. Your Scattered Hairs partner may have no problem with this, but if you do, you may want to fix your focus. Set your sights on your partner's gifts and take care of your own brows.

STRAYS AT END

When stray hairs form a single broken line at an eyebrow's *very end*, curiosity is revealed. Strays at End suggest an individual who asks a lot of questions. When seen at the very end of a *thin* eyebrow, this suggests an individual who *wants* to ask a lot of questions, but who may not ask them.

LONG WILD HAIRS

Long eyebrow hairs growing upward and outward are Long Wild Hairs. They reveal a mind searching for unusual answers; these individuals have a gift for coming up with unconventional ideas. These eyebrows are sometimes referred to as "Mad Scientist Eyebrows." When Long Wild Hairs are seen at the eyebrow's beginning, middle, and end, it shows one whose mind is very active from inception to completion of goals and projects.

Long Wild Hairs Individuals think in a different way than most people. Most often found on older men, these hairs indicate talent for invention and ingenuity. Long Wild Hairs Individuals enjoy fixing things and figuring things out. Their uncommon solutions, however, are not always as brilliant, or as practical, as they might think. And sometimes these individuals complicate simple matters.

If looking for someone who might love helping you find answers to your puzzling problems, look for an individual with Long Wild Hairs. Even if the individual's solution is weird or unworkable, his or her desire to help can be looked upon as a loving gesture.

STICK-UP, START-UP HAIRS

When hairs stick straight up at the start of the brow they are Stick-Up, Start-Up Hairs. Stick-Up, Start-Up Hairs reveals a gift for solving problems before others are aware that a problem needs to be solved.

You may think your partner with Stick Up, Start-Up Hairs is intuitive, seeing future problems before they exist. Or, you may think your partner is just looking for problems, when in your mind there are none.

Orderly brows, orderly thoughts

Eyebrow hairs may grow in an orderly fashion, with all going in the same direction, or they may grow in different directions. Eyebrow hair direction reveals *clarity of thought*.

Same Direction Hairs

Different Direction Hairs

SAME DIRECTION HAIRS

Eyebrow hairs growing the in the same direction are Same Direction Hairs. Same Direction Hairs tell of organized thoughts and clarity of mind. This is even more likely when eyebrows are well shaped.

Same Direction Hairs suggest clear thinking, making it easier to accomplish goals and realize desires. Emotions are more likely balanced and sexual passions have a better chance of being under control. The more elegant the brow, the more cultured an individual tends to be.

The orderliness of the Same Direction Hairs brings the ability to teach in a way easy to follow. If lengthy instruction is needed, seek out an individual with eyebrows that are orderly, long, dark, and thick. If only quick and clear instruction is required, the eyebrows just need to be orderly.

A Same Direction Hairs Individual might have an easier time being faithful due to the clarity of mind and control of passions suggested in these eyebrows. But if drunk on alcohol or stoned on drugs, this person's sensibility will be dulled like anyone else's.

DIFFERENT DIRECTION HAIRS

Eyebrow hairs growing in different directions are Different Direction Hairs and indicate thoughts going in different directions. Some Different Direction Hairs Individuals can deal with many disparate thoughts without difficulty, but others are hampered by a lack of clear direction. Different Direction Hairs may tell of a confused mind, but can also reveal a gift for creativity and innovative ideas.

Different Direction Hairs have a messy look and some with these brows live and work in disorganized surroundings. They have more important things on their minds. When *thick*, they are the eyebrows of inventors. When *very long*, this indicates wild, unconventional ideas. Different Direction Hairs Individuals who are less impulsive have an easier time dealing with the potential challenges their brows present.

If surroundings are neat and organized, thoughts have an easier time being focused and clear. If your partner has Different Direction Hairs and you have Same Direction Hairs, you might help by straightening out the living environment. But, be sure to ask your partner's permission before tossing things out. Some people find comfort in clutter. Make certain your partner is okay with you organizing his or her belongings before you begin.

A Different Direction Hairs date may emit mixed signals, moving forward and then back. Confusion may be contagious. Be clear about what you want.

Feel the feel for feelings

Eyebrows may feel soft, stiff, or somewhere in between. Eyebrow hair strength reveals *commitment to convictions.*

STIFF EYEBROW HAIRS

When eyebrow hairs are unbendable, they are Stiff Eyebrow Hairs. They suggest passion, strength, and vitality; gifts that are enhanced when hairs are dark and thick. Stiff Eyebrow Hairs Individuals tend not to be easy going. Stiff Eyebrow Hairs are strong hairs and reveal strong commitment to convictions.

Stiff Eyebrow Hairs also suggest assertive individuals who don't back down. These hairs indicate the challenge of rigid thinking but bring strength for fighting causes and for leadership.

If your date has Stiff Eyebrow Hairs he or she is not likely to let go of an issue that he or she wants to discuss.

SOFT EYEBROW HAIRS

Soft Eyebrow Hairs suggest a gentle spirit and cooperative nature, which is more likely to be true when the eyebrows themselves are thin. Because Soft Eyebrow Hairs suggest less vitality than hairs with more body to them, these individuals may need to monitor energy expenditure. The fact that these individuals tend to give in easily might be attributable in part to lack of energy.

Soft Eyebrow Hairs reveal individuals less opinionated and more open to hearing thoughts of others. Soft Eyebrow Hairs suggest one has an easier time putting aside judgments and old beliefs, allowing for new information and new ideas to enter. These individuals tend to be less committed to convictions, which can be seen as a challenge or a gift.

Soft Eyebrow Hairs Individuals most often are quite sensitive to others. Many have a calm exterior but can have emotions that may be unpredictable, as well as little bursts of anger from time to time. They tend, however, not to harbor angry feelings.

Your Soft Eyebrow Hairs partner may have said some things during a sudden "anger snap." If your partner apologized with sincerity, it is up to you to decide to let go and forgive or hold on to a grudge.

THE EYEBROW RIDGE

Some people have a well-defined horizontal ridge that divides the eyebrows from the forehead. This is a showing of the brow bone and reveals a strong drive, leadership ability, rigid thinking, and a high level of testosterone. The Eyebrow Ridge corresponds to the Wood element.

A defined ridge shows a desire to be the authority

An Eyebrow Ridge doesn't stand out on everyone, but if it does it may be merely observable or obviously prominent. *Very* prominent ridges are boney looking and found only on men. Eyebrow Ridges reveal *assertion of power.*

OBSERVABLE RIDGE

A slightly noticeable ridge is an Observable Ridge. Observable Ridges suggest rigid thinkers who have challenges being flexible and often have self-imposed beliefs about life and love.

Observable Ridge Individuals believe in rules and proven procedures. Following them gives a sense of control and helps determine outcome. They like working this way, think it is the "right way" and want others to work this way as well.

Some of the rules and procedures they follow are not known to others but are those they devised. Challenges might arise when these individuals are too rigid or when others don't view them as an authority. Nevertheless, the Observable Ridge can be a gift for reaching goals due to a no-nonsense approach and strong drive.

Observable Ridge Individuals desire to assert their power and authority when it comes to how things should be done. For example, you may be driving your Observable Ridge date somewhere and, upon arriving at the desired destination, you stop the car and reach over to hug. Your Observable Ridge date says, "Hugging is done standing up!" for this is the correct way to hug in your date's rule book. What to do? Some possible choices: (1) Get out of the car with your date so you can hug "properly"; (2) let your date out of the car, say "goodbye," and drive off; (3) ignore what you think is a stupid rigid rule and (attempt to) give a hug anyway. What you do may reveal *your* possible control issues.

PROMINENT BONEY RIDGE

A ridge with a bonier look is a Prominent Boney Ridge. A Prominent Boney Ridge reveals tremendous physical presence, incredible drive, and a strong desire to assert power. These individuals need to be the authority.

Prominent Boney Ridge Individuals are natural leaders. In business they have a talent for maximizing workplace efficiency. Due to low tolerance for those ineffective or weak, they find it challenging working with lazy, unproductive people. Prominent Boney Ridge Individuals thrive on challenges and their strong drive is an asset in reaching goals. A Prominent Boney Ridge suggests a high level of testosterone. One with a Prominent Boney Ridge is often gifted as an athlete.

To make the most of a romantic three-day getaway, a Prominent Boney Ridge partner may assert his power and maximize efficiency by putting a solid plan of action into place. A detailed itinerary may be provided with wake-up times and times and locations of all meals. What to eat may be planned as well. Activities and their times may be laid out in advance and alternative plans prepared in the event weather interferes.

In dating situations, a man with a Prominent Boney Ridge will need to control the speed of a developing relationship. If you are wondering how a Prominent Boney Ridge man is "feeling" about you, the question is how he is "thinking" about you, as Prominent Boney Ridge Individuals come from a thinking rather than feeling place.

THE EYELIDS

Eyelids reveal desire for connection or may show a natural feeling of connection. They suggest how open a person is to letting others into his or her life, or into his or her conversation. Eyelids also can reveal stagnation or an accumulation of some sort. Upper eyelids correspond to the Earth element. Lower eyelids correspond to the Water element. Bottom rims correspond to the Wood element.

Connection can be found in no fold

Eyelids are single or double. Single Eyelids have no fold. Double Eyelids have a fold, but on some eyes the fold is difficult to see. Upper eyelids reveal *feelings of connection.*

SINGLE EYELIDS

A Single Eyelid has no fold. It has a "straight connection" between the eyebrow and eye and suggests a natural feeling of being connected to others.

Single Eyelids Individuals have a gift when it comes to seeing the interconnected nature of all life. They tend to enjoy sharing, belonging, and doing things with other people. Single Eyelids suggest connection, but do not tell how quickly one wants to get close. Look to the eyebrows for clues about this.

A Single Eyelids date may want others to join the two of you when you go out. You might have to share time with this person. More time could be needed before getting close.

DOUBLE EYELIDS

When there is a fold between the eyebrow and eye, it is a Double Eyelid. Double Eyelids suggest a feeling of being separate and apart from others. Double Eyelids Individuals have varying degrees of desire for connection, and this is revealed by the amount of space between the eye and eyelid fold.

Eyelids expose intimacy requirements

Double Eyelids expose the level of desire for connection and intimacy. Eyelid exposure tends to stay the same from day to day, but temporary puffiness can occur, blurring the exposure. Keep this in mind when meeting someone for the first time. To obtain a correct reading, check eyelids on more than one occasion.

Single Eyelids tell of a natural feeling of connection but do not reveal intimacy requirements. *Eyelid exposure described below corresponds to Double Eyelids only*. The greater the space between the eyelid and the fold the more the eyelid is "exposed." Double Eyelid "exposure" reveals *desire to bond*.

EYELIDS VERY EXPOSED

When there is a large space between the eye and the fold, the eyelid is an Eyelid Very Exposed. Eyelids Very Exposed reveal a strong desire for closeness and a desire to bond quickly.

These individuals tend to be action oriented with speed useful for getting things done. These eyelids tell of a desire not to over-analyze and a preference for just enough information to grasp a concept and know what's going on.

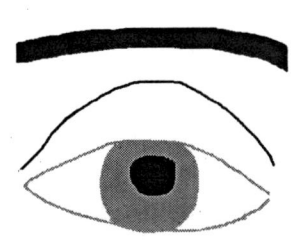

Eyelid Very
Exposed

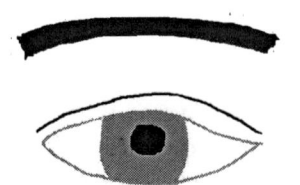

Eyelid Moderately
Exposed

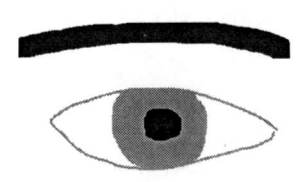

Eyelid Not Exposed

The fast action revealed in these eyelids is beneficial in jobs requiring a fast pace. However, these individuals sometimes cut others off in mid-sentence in order to hurry things up. They don't always wait to hear all the facts. They cut short potentially long conversations. Furthermore, Eyelids Very Exposed Individuals often are in a hurry to get into a relationship. To them, being in one is very important. Impatience is a possible challenge for them.

If you are out with an Eyelids Very Exposed Individual on a first date, you may not be asked too many questions. There may be no need to go into details. Eyelids Very Exposed suggest a desire for quick connection and intimacy. If you are okay with this, deeper questions concerning compatibility can be dealt with at another time.

Couples with Eyelids Very Exposed tend to find it challenging to be apart for long.

EYELIDS MODERATELY EXPOSED

A moderate space between the eyelid and fold reveals an Eyelid Moderately Exposed. Moderate exposure indicates a mid-range desire for connection and a basic want for bonding. Eyelids Moderately Exposed Individuals tend to desire the closeness that comes with a relationship, but exhibit some resistance before becoming involved. They take a sensible approach. They need enough information first.

Perhaps your partner *had* Eyelids Moderately Exposed, but *now has no exposure. Eyelids Not Exposed* suggest a need for personal space. Newly unexposed eyelids may not mean that you partner has lost interest, but may just mean your partner has been working very hard and temporarily has less energy for being intimate. Putting pressure on your partner could press the eyelids down further and might also push your partner away.

EYELIDS NOT EXPOSED

When you can't see the fold, or at least not much of it, the eyelid is an Eyelid Not Exposed. Eyelids Not Exposed suggest a need for independence and a tendency to overanalyze.

Eyelids Not Exposed Individuals are self-contained; they require personal space. They have a low level of desire to bond; they take their time and move slowly. To be in a relationship, it needs to be just right, and what is right for them might be a "loosely based relationship." Eyelids Not Exposed Individuals cut off clinging individuals. Work is often very important to them and often is their focus. These eyelids reveal the gift of the ability to focus as well.

If your date has Eyelids Not Exposed and *lower eyelids* that form a *straight* line this reveals he or she screens information carefully. If you want to be "let in" you will have to build trust. If interested in this individual, be patient.

A single individual with Eyelids Not Exposed will not want a relationship with a person who he or she feels is co-dependent. And, if a single individual with Eyelids Not Exposed says he or she is not interested in a relationship, believe what he or she says.

Puffs indicate a need to let go

Upper eyelids may be puffy, and some droop as well. Eyelid puffs reveal *stagnation of some sort*.

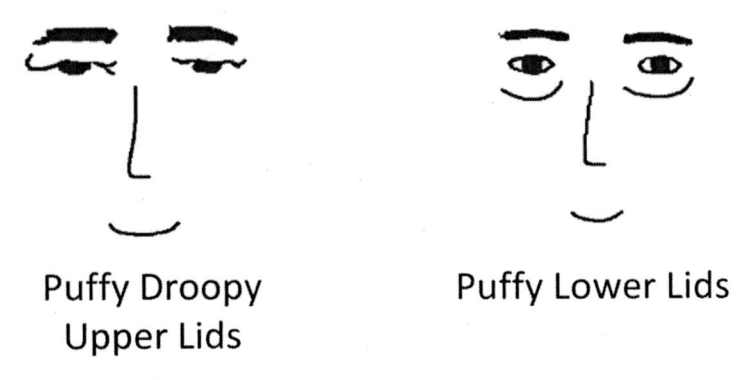

Puffy Droopy Upper Lids

Puffy Lower Lids

PUFFY UPPER LIDS

Upper eyelids that are *puffy* are Puffy Upper Lids. Puffy Upper Lids tell of accumulation due to stagnation of some sort. Also, Puffy Upper Lids can reveal a build-up of irritation. Irritation may be due to dealing with "challenging" people, or the irritation may stem from one's environment. Keep in mind, too, that Puffy Upper Lids can be a temporary swelling due to an allergic reaction or may be puffy from lack of sleep.

Puffy Upper Lids are also found on analytical types who ask a lot of questions. An analytical mind is a gift and analytical individuals can excel working as researchers, technicians, investigators, and can use their gift in many other "questioning type" positions. However, a need to investigate can sometimes overcomplicate simple matters. Puffy Upper Lids might tell that too many thoughts have accumulated and thinking is stagnated. Puffy Upper Lids Individuals often have the challenge of letting go of the need to know everything first.

Only the left eyelid being puffy stems from something in an individual's personal life. Only the right eyelid being puffy is likely due to business, professional, or financial reasons.

Puffy Upper Lids can also reveal people who set their sights on accumulating money and are good at it. The ability to hold on to assets is a gift, but if this behavior is excessive, it can be a challenge. Puffy Upper Lids can indicate stagnation of energy around wealth.

PUFFY DROOPY LIDS

An upper eyelid that sags or hangs down over the eye, and is also puffy, is a Puffy Droopy Lid. Puffy Droopy Lids often reveal a hard worker and this can be a commendable trait. Hard workers tend to be responsible, security minded, and determined. Some, however, work too hard and are workaholics.

Puffy Droopy Lids can also suggest an excessive worrier who does not have enough pleasure in life. Too much heavy thinking weighs the lids down and can put an individual in a bad mood. Some Puffy Droopy Lids Individuals have been in a bad mood for some time.

An individual with Puffy Droopy Lids can be touchy and defensive. These lids often reveal a person whose life is stagnating to some degree, or at least in his or her mind. Getting out of the head, or out of the office or house, might be beneficial for a Puffy Droopy Lids Individual.

Eyelids that hang but are not puffy are just droopy and can be due to age. Ear bottoms, nose bottoms, chin bottoms, and bottoms in general, droop over time.

If you see Puffy Droopy Lids on your partner, this suggests a feeling of weariness. You may think it would be good for him or her to get away for some pleasure and fun. Remember, you can't change your partner, who may be happiest when working hard, or may feel it is his or her responsibility to do so.

PUFFY LOWER LIDS

When lower lids are puffy, they are Puffy Lower Lids. They may also be referred to as "Eye Bags." These are commonly caused by allergies, lack of sleep, or too much salt in a diet. When Puffy Lower Lids show a hint of brownish-green this suggests one holding on to frustration. When light blue this indicates a person is working too hard and depleting the adrenals. Lower lids that are puffy not due to reasons given above can reveal a holding on to sadness with the inability to shed tears.

If you have Puffy Lower Lids and have been grieving or have been very sad, but you have not been expressing your emotions, you may find that the puffiness disappears by releasing the pent-up pain through tears.

The eyes are open, but are you being let in?

The rims of lower eyelids tell of openness to others, to information, or to the environment. Rounder on children and younger individuals, lower eyelids straighten with age. The rims of an adult's lower lids tend to stay about the same from day to day. But, if rims change while interacting with another individual, it indicates a change in receptivity. A change in receptivity can either round or straighten the rims of the lower lids. A lower eyelid's curve reveals *degree of openness*.

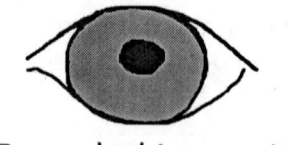

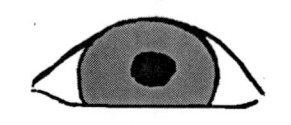

ROUND LOWER LIDS

Round Lower Lids are those that are curved. A Round Lower Lid reveals the person is "letting in." How much depends on the amount of the curve.

Round Lower Lids reveal approachable, receptive individuals open to other people and new ideas. Round Lower Lids suggest a trusting open heart, concern for others, and one who gives thought to others when making decisions. These individuals tend to communicate with kindness. Those with these lids, however, may have the challenge of being overly sensitive or emotionally vulnerable. Very Round Lower Lids can tell of innocence.

When dating it may be helpful to know that when your date's lower lids become rounder while the two of you are interacting, this indicates increased interest. Look for an increase in the curve! But, if you are in a relationship and notice your partner's lower lids becoming rounder while talking with another person, there is no need to become reactive or alarmed. This simply can mean your partner is very interested in the topic of conversation or is open to learning something new.

STRAIGHT LOWER LIDS

When lower lids are straight, they are Straight Lower Lids. Straight Lower Lids show restraint in opening up and getting close. It is important that these individuals feel comfortable first.

Straight Lower Lids tell of logic, reason, and common sense in dealing with others and in making decisions. These individuals tend to be competitive and play to win; this can benefit them in business dealings. Straight Lower Lids Individuals give careful thought to matters of the heart.

Some with Straight Lower Lids are social and friendly when it comes to superficial relationships, but close up when someone wants more. Others with Straight Lower Lids are naturally somewhat introverted individuals who guard their emotions and thoughts. And other individuals had at one time been open but have been very hurt and are now very cautious.

You can only have deep, loving *interaction* with a person who is open to receiving. If you have Round Lower Lids, a Straight Lower Lids Individual may not want the same depth of relationship that you do.

RAISED LOWER LIDS

When the lower lid is raised, such that the bottom of the eye is cut off, it is a Raised Lower Lid. Raised Lower Lids suggest some closure to the "Window of the Soul." One may be hiding something or one's entire self. Only the *left* eye having a Raised Lower Lid indicates hiding emotions. If only the *right* lower lid is raised, this could tell of hiding a physical act or desire. Raised Lower Lids sometimes disclose an extreme need to retreat, to withdraw, or to protect the heart for reasons the individual may not be entirely conscious of. Raised Lower Lids suggest one who, at least in the moment, is not open to opening up.

If your partner has lower eyelids that you notice have recently risen, it might have nothing to do with you. Your partner may have recently revealed much more than he or she feels comfortable revealing—at work or to others—and may be pulling back and pulling up the eyelids temporarily. The Raised Lower Lids in this case would suggest a protective nature and a temporary hiding of self. To see if your partner might be hiding something else, look to the eyes to see if they are shifty.

Lower eyelids can rise suddenly when a person starts to get angry and tenses up. If you see this happen, take it as a warning of what might be coming.

THE EYES

Considered "Windows of the Soul," eyes show general attitude and outlook; inner energy and emotional openness. Eyes give clues to stress level, honesty, and focus. And, the health of an individual may also be seen. More open in youth, eyes narrow with life experiences. Women tend to have larger eyes than men. Eyes correspond to the Fire element, but, vision and eye depth correspond to Wood.

Lines extending from the outer corners of eyes are called "smile lines" or "crow's feet." Although often unwanted, they reveal charisma, joy, and the ability to attract the opposite sex, or same sex, as the case may be. They bring a gift for making sales and closing business deals. When these lines extend horizontally, and then curve up, extra magnetism is revealed. These lines bring the above gifts but also reveal greater potential for infidelity due to their strong ability to attract.

Eye size shows the size of the heart's opening

To determine eye size, focus on the vertical height but also consider the horizontal width. Look at the eyes' size in proportion to the face. The way lids are held can change the eyes' appearance. Narrowing lids make eyes appear smaller. Eye size reveals *emotional openness*.

Small Eyes

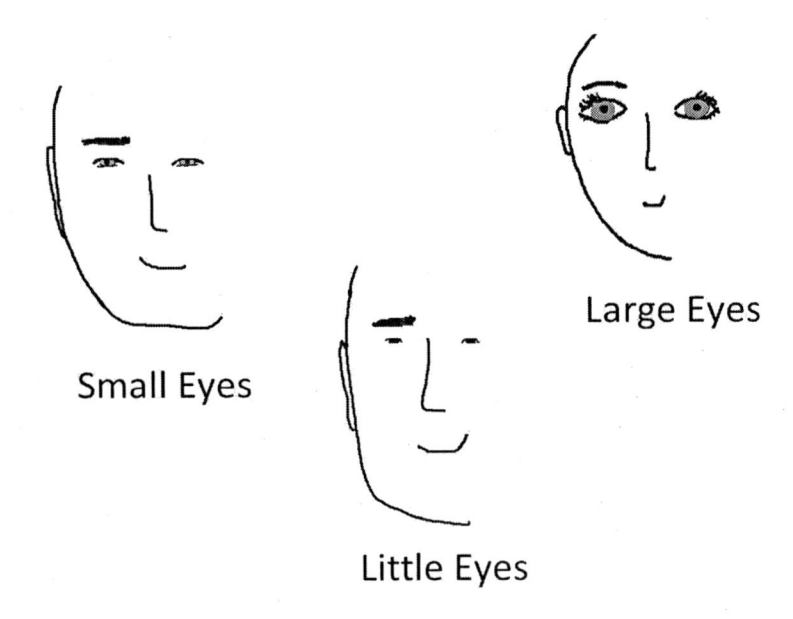

Large Eyes

Little Eyes

LARGE EYES

Large Eyes are tall, wide, and "open." They tell of a trusting heart. The *rounder* the Large Eyes, the more open one is to letting others in.

Large Eyes reveal expressive, receptive, open-minded individuals who are quicker to take a chance on love and have an easier time accepting things without questioning or requiring proof. They trust, have difficulty hiding lies, and may have trouble keeping secrets.

Large Eyes Individuals tend to fall in love easily with interest difficult to conceal. Some have the challenges of being gullible, impulsive, or naïve. They may not want to believe all people are not safe to let in. Narrowing their eyes by lowering their lids can slow things down, giving them more time to get to know a person or to evaluate a situation. Sunglasses can also be useful for this purpose. They feel deeply and might be hurt easily when feelings are not mutual.

Large Eyes Individuals are ideally suited for work in which they can be expressive and creative. They excel when taking a visual or hands-on approach and are more receptive to information when it is seen. Listening without eye contact can be challenging for them. Detailed instructions are best understood when written.

Vitality and a passionate nature are revealed in Large Eyes. They show a high level of inner energy; when used intelligently this brings success. These eyes get noticed and notice others; entertainers and leaders benefit from having expressive Large Eyes. When *very bright*, however, this tells of intense energy and one who may be aggressive in getting his or her needs met.

Dating? If you have Large Eyes and are asked to go away on a romantic getaway—with no strings attached—you best think twice. (Or at least give it some thought before responding. Large Eyes Individuals are known to speak before they think.) If you go away with an individual you are attracted to, you are likely to want more. An individual with smaller eyes tends not to open his or her heart as quickly and may be able to take a weekend away with no commitment. For you, a romantic fling with someone who interests you a great deal, but who you may or may not see again, probably won't work.

SMALL EYES

Small Eyes look small compared to the size of the face. Some are short, some are long, but all Small Eyes are narrow.

Small Eyes suggest tight control of feelings and those who are introspective and cautious. Small Eyes Individuals have a talent for blocking out emotional distractions; this can benefit them in business. They tend not to waste emotional energy; this helps reach goals and get things done. Small Eyes bring the gifts of logic, reason, and attention to detail. These Individuals are analytical and like to think.

Small Eyes indicate protection around the heart which can pose challenges to intimacy in relationships. Small Eyes Individuals do not fall in love easily, but if they do they typically fall hard. Once they commit they can be very committed and devoted.

Dating a Small Eyes Individual to whom you would like to get close requires patience. They take time to open their heart to another. Some never open up their heart enough to let another in fully. A relationship might be more surface than deep. And this works perfectly for some people.

LITTLE EYES

Little Eyes are narrower and shorter than Small Eyes. They are tiny when compared to the size of the face. Little Eyes Individuals often hold back saying what they think. Their emotions are hidden from others, and some Little Eyes Individuals are not all that in touch with how they feel themselves. When it comes to emotional openness, they tend to be quite closed.

Little Eyes Individuals have a gift for details and scrutinizing people, situations, and things. These eyes may be put to good use in positions requiring examining or investigating various matters. Little Eyes Individuals don't trust easily but are trustworthy individuals good at keeping secrets. Eyes *very little* might disclose self-centered ambition.

Little Eyes Individuals place extreme importance on keeping private matters private. If your partner has Little Eyes, give thought to his or her nature before speaking about the details of your relationship to others. And, there are likely some things your partner does not want even *you* to know.

For point of view, look where the eye points

Not all eyes are set in a horizontal straight line. Some slant up, some slant down. An eye's angle reveals *outlook on life*.

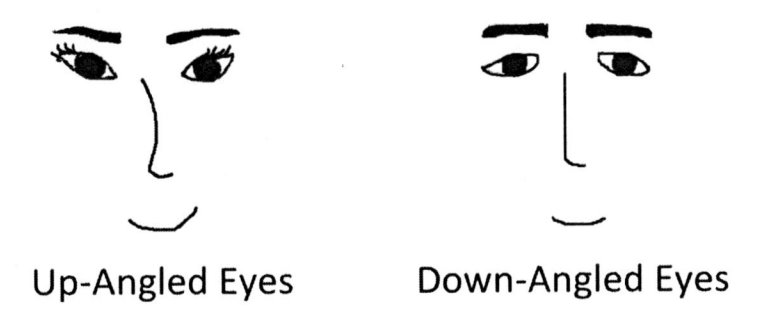

Up-Angled Eyes   **Down-Angled Eyes**

UP-ANGLED EYES

When the eye's outer corner is higher than the inner, the eye slants up and is an Up-Angled Eye. Up-Angled Eyes suggest an optimistic outlook on life. Up-Angled Eyes Individuals look for the best in people and situations; they spot opportunities easily. They are enthusiastic about enjoying life.

Their expectancy of good can attract success in business and bring prosperity. They go after goals that others don't even think of attempting. They have a gift for up-lifting others but some people are turned off by their sunny disposition. Some see them as unrealistic.

If you are attracted to a positive personality, you may view your Up-Angled Eyes partner as being attractive in more ways than one.

If you have Up-Angled Eyes and are in the early stages of a relationship, you may see only the positive. However, perhaps the relationship is not quite right; your partner may not be a good fit, but that is not your focus. Although it is true that the more one looks for good, the more one sees, in some situations your challenge might be to look at the facts and not what you would prefer to believe.

DOWN-ANGLED EYES

When the outer corner is lower than the inner, the eye slants down and is a Down-Angled Eye. Down-Angled Eyes suggest a somewhat negative outlook on life. These individuals do not get as enthusiastic about things as others might. Their eyes show honesty, helpfulness, gentleness, understanding, and possibly sadness as well.

Down-Angled Eyes tell of a realistic perspective that some people view as pessimistic. It is just that Down-Angled Eyes Individuals know that people disappoint, situations don't always turn out the way they want, and life is not always pretty. Most are sensible and practical individuals others can relate to. They anticipate trouble, allowing them to address problems before they occur or escalate.

Some negative, gloomy talking Down-Angled Eyes Individuals can keep others away, but others with these eyes have a gift for drawing people to them. Their real-life understanding can be a blessing to others.

Those who have grown through difficult life experiences can be a source of comfort, help, and inspiration to those going through a tough time.

A Down-Angled Eyes date is likely to be a serious person. He or she might also be very compassionate with a heart that will understand and ears that will listen. (The length of ears might tell you how long.)

Your Down-Angled Eyes partner can easily see drawbacks, difficulties, and glitches. You may think if your partner stopped looking for problems, he or she would find less of them. If your partner's approach is working, however, your partner does not view it as a problem. In certain situations involving you, see your partner's outlook as looking out for you.

Spacing shows span of focus

Some people have eyes spaced closely together; others have eyes spaced far apart. When looking at spacing, evaluate eyes to see if they appear more in the center or closer to the sides of the face. Eye spacing suggests *tolerance*.

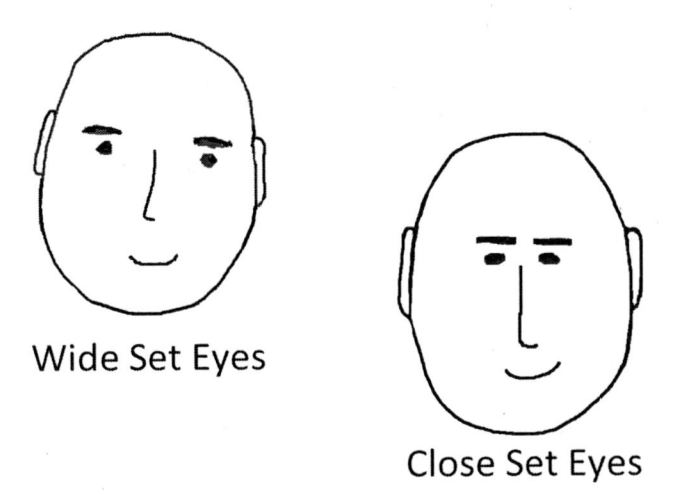

Wide Set Eyes

Close Set Eyes

WIDE SET EYES

When eyes are closer to the sides than to the vertical center of a face, they are Wide Set Eyes. Wide Set Eyes reveal a broad perspective and tell of tolerance. Wide Set Eyes Individuals have an easier time seeing the big picture and tend to be accepting of people, situations, and things. These eyes reveal the ability to see the reasons behind actions, circumstances, and words. However, because of their high degree of tolerance, Wide Set Eyes Individuals are sometimes misled, imposed upon, or deceived.

Other challenges can arise when it comes to concentration, focus, or details. An accountant a Wide Set Eyes Individual was not meant to be! If a writer, this person will need a proofreader, as he or she is likely to have difficulty catching all mistakes and may often leave out words. Yet, Wide Set Eyes Individuals have potential to excel at speed reading, because they have a greater ability to see and grasp the basic meaning of entire sentences at a time. Wide Set Eyes can often also tell of artistic gifts.

Wide Set Eyes reveal broadmindedness and those more likely to be accepting of different types of people, different ways of thinking, and different forms of relationships. They tend to be easy to get along with. Some with eyes spaced *very wide*, however, have the potential to be too carefree about relationships.

If you have Wide Set Eyes, take care not to be naïve. With a naturally open-minded viewpoint you may sometimes tolerate more than you should. When dating someone new, you might be unable to see the little red flags of warning right in front of you.

If you reject a Wide Set Eyes Individual's request for a date, he or she might view your rejection from a broader perspective. Wide Set Eyes Individuals can have an easier time than others accepting the idea that people are sometimes *lucky* when they don't get what they want.

CLOSE SET EYES

Eyes closer to the vertical center of the face than to the sides are Close Set Eyes. They show centered vision and a gift for focus and details. Close Set Eyes Individuals view life from a somewhat limited perspective, like to work independently, and are often impatient to succeed.

Close Set Eyes Individuals can block out distractions easily and concentrate on the task at hand. They excel at research and detailed work and have the ability to spot errors quickly. They inspect things carefully, which is useful assessing business situations and going over the fine points of technical or legal documents. Close Set Eyes bring a gift for focusing on the goal ahead, but the potential challenge of focusing on faults in others.

Close Set Eyes Individuals tend to use caution when it comes to taking risks. Before becoming too involved, a Close Set Eyes Individual is likely to scrutinize a potential relationship. Close Set Eyes Individuals examine everything carefully.

If your partner has Close Set Eyes, he or she has the ability to spot errors quickly. Your partner might be easily irritated or impatient with you at times. This often will have less to do with you than it does with your partner's natural focus. If your eyes are Wide Set, focus on the big picture to see the gifts of your partner's Close Set Eyes.

If you have Close Set Eyes, consider the fact that criticism, when given to be helpful, is received more easily.

Depth discloses eagerness to relate

Eyes may be deep in the sockets or may appear to be more "out front." Most reside somewhere in the middle. Eye depth reveals *eagerness to participate in life.*

Deep Set Eyes

Bulging Eyes

DEEP SET EYES

Eyes positioned deep in the sockets are Deep Set Eyes. Deep Set Eyes suggest a "holding back" when it comes to participating in life. These individuals have an observant, reflective nature and an easier time taking things in than letting things out. Considerable thought precedes the actions they take and the words they speak.

When it comes to work, Deep Set Eyes Individuals need to make good use of their mind. They are often drawn to careers involving research, art, philosophy, inventing, or writing of some sort.

These eyes suggest a mysterious individual. Many people are attracted to those with Deep Set Eyes, and they can attract many lovers. When it comes to a serious relationship, they rarely move fast.

Deep Set Eyes Individuals may appear calm and relaxed but are often intense beneath the surface. They need time alone to reflect. Too much time alone, however, brings the possibility of becoming reclusive. A dark cast seen around Deep Set Eyes can reveal a depressed individual.

Your Deep Set Eyes partner may seem more critical than those individuals with eyes not deep set. This can be due to deep thinking. Deep Set Eyes Individuals are analytical and excel at finding answers to problems that others not as introspective might miss. Hear what your partner says, and you may see things differently.

If you have eyes set at a *moderate depth* and have just had a date with someone with Deep Set Eyes, you may realize that participation in conversation about personal matters was unequal. It is a Deep Set Eyes Individual's nature to open up slowly, while those with eyes set at a *moderate depth* open up at a moderate speed. And, if you have "*Bulging Eyes*," it is not your nature to hold back. On a first date a *Bulging Eyes* Individual might reveal very personal information, such as the most intimate details of past relationships.

Deep Set Eyes Individuals do not initially disclose feelings and private matters, but some, when newly interested in someone, may answer personal questions if they are asked. Although they may seem to open up, they are not likely to divulge details. They aren't eager to explain some things.

BULGING EYES

Eyes that appear to bulge out from the sockets are Bulging Eyes. They suggest an eagerness to participate in life. Bulging Eyes Individuals reach out to others with their eyes, arms, and emotions. One reason a person may have Bulging Eyes is an overactive thyroid condition. Others have Bulging Eyes without an underlying medical problem.

Bulging Eyes indicate a nervous way of being in the world. You may find these individuals making sudden changes in their career, residence, or relationships, as well as taking chances. Many bring excitement to their work and their life and have the ability to draw people to them. But, many others with Bulging Eyes have an anxious, penetrating way of looking out; creating uneasiness that keeps others away. This can bring up challenges for these individuals who desire so much to be included.

When it comes to relationships, most Bulging Eyes Individuals want to jump right in. In a relationship, it is important for them to be noticed and feel appreciated. When hurt or criticized they shut down.

Another reason for Bulging Eyes reveals different character traits. These individuals also have *dilated pupils*. These eyes reveal hypersensitive individuals who were likely traumatized, often early in life. Bulging Eyes Individuals of this type keep their eyes wide, staying alert and on guard. Unlike enthusiastic, outgoing Bulging Eyes Individuals, they are introverted and quiet. They are tense and can be jumpy. They are often reactive, but strive to stay balanced.

An individual with Bulging Eyes due to the lookout for danger, such as the type described in the paragraph above, will greatly benefit from a calm environment and an understanding partner. A stable, loving relationship can help a Bulging Eyes Individual of this nature feel safe. Over time, this might allow the eyes to retreat in the socket and relax in the face.

Eye shapes tell of time spent thinking

Basic eye shapes are Round, Oval, Almond, Narrow, and Rectangular. Some eyes appear smaller or narrower due to the narrowing of the lids.

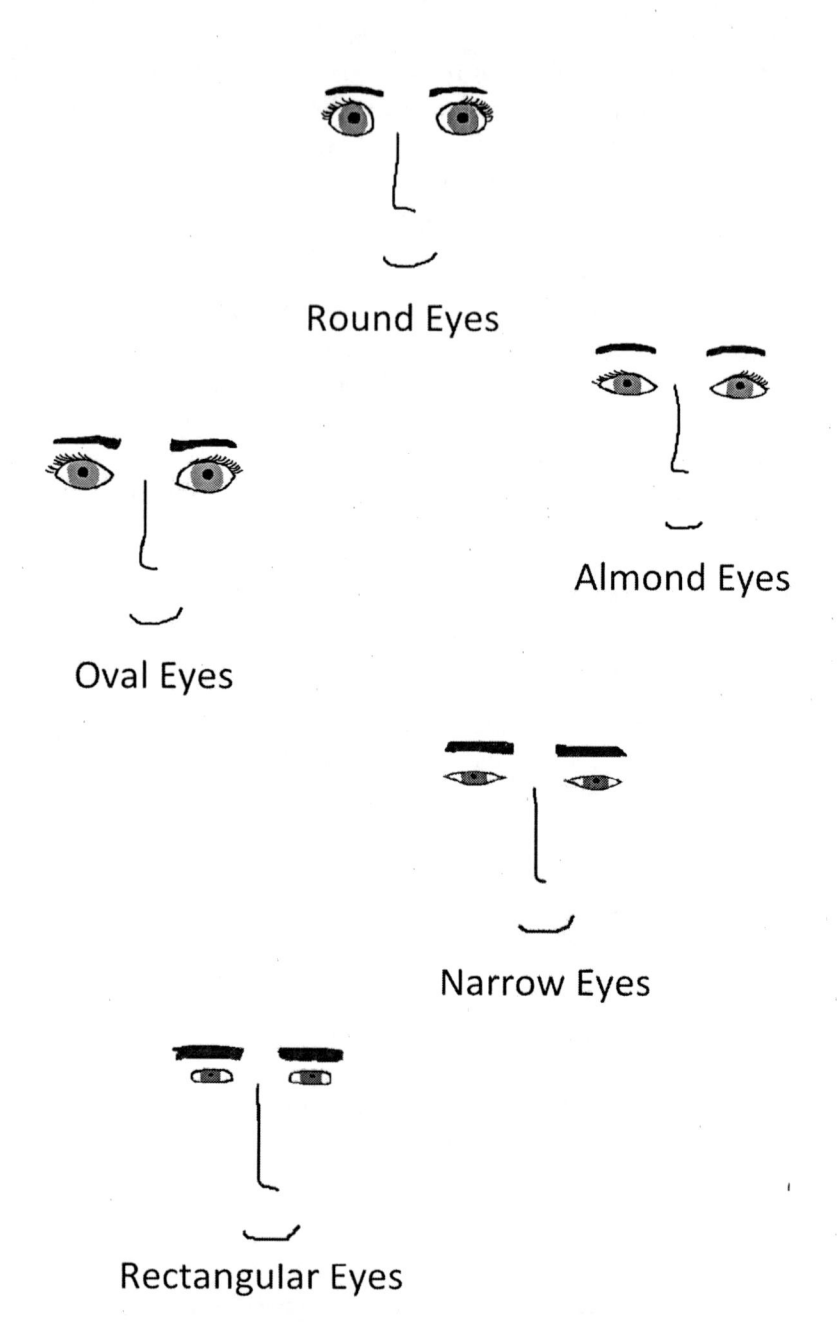

Round Eyes

Almond Eyes

Oval Eyes

Narrow Eyes

Rectangular Eyes

The larger the eyes appear, the more emotionally open an individual will tend to be. The lids give shape to the eyes. Eye shapes reveal *time spent thinking before speaking.*

ROUND EYES

Round Eyes are nearly as high as they are wide and are round in shape. Round Eyes Individuals tend to spend little time thinking before speaking and at times speak before they think. The larger the eyes, the more likely this is to be the case. Round Eyes suggest an emotional nature and artistic tendencies. Round Eyes Individuals speak from the heart with feeling. Those more reserved might call them bold.

Round Eyes Individuals love to be in love. Concerning work, it is important they love what they do. Concerning relationships, they tend to get involved easily.

Your date with large Round Eyes may jump right into a conversation with personal questions. He or she may not hesitate saying what is on his or her mind. Depending on your nature, you may find your date's childlike directness charming and refreshing, or you may be uncomfortable with his or her straightforwardness.

OVAL EYES

Oval Eyes are similar to Round Eyes but are longer horizontally. Oval Eyes Individuals tend to spend more time thinking before speaking than those with Round Eyes. They tone down their approach and their words. The larger the eyes, the more emotional one will tend to be. Many find success in creative or visual fields.

If you are trying to communicate something to your Oval Eyes partner, your chances will improve if you make constant eye contact while speaking. (The same holds true for one with Round Eyes.)

ALMOND EYES

Almond Eyes are of medium height with a long horizontal width. They have a slight curve on top and bottom; as their name implies, their shape is similar to that of an almond. When it comes to expressing themselves, Almond Eyes Individuals spend a balanced amount of time thinking before speaking. Almond Eyes reveal an open but somewhat restrained individual. Some people view them as mysterious.

Almond Eyes Individuals are not ruled by emotions. They think things through before expressing themselves and use common sense before committing to a relationship. They tend to have a high degree of skepticism and distrust in their nature, which when used wisely serves them well.

Almond Eyes Individuals may date a little longer or date more than one person simultaneously before settling down. This is not due to being a "player" and might have nothing to do with a lack of desire for commitment. Instead, it is due to a cautious approach.

NARROW EYES

Narrow Eyes are short in height. Long or moderate in length, the *curve* on the top and bottom is minimal.

Narrow Eyes see out, but others can't see in. When it comes to revealing personal information, time is taken before speaking and often little is revealed. Narrow Eyes suggest a strong, active constitution along with sound judgment and a need for privacy. Some with this eye shape have a heart that is closed due to being hurt badly in the past.

Narrow Eyes are a blessing in situations that require a high level of confidentiality. They often bring a gift for details, useful in many types of positions. And, because it is difficult to read these people, poker players benefit from having Narrow Eyes.

Are you interested in a Narrow Eyes Individual? If you say in a loving way, "I want to know all about you" don't be surprised if he or she replies, "I will tell you only what I want you to know." And, if you are already in a relationship with a Narrow Eyes Individual, he or she may still only tell you what he or she wants you to know.

A Narrow Eyes Individual feels it is very important that one thinks before one speaks. Others who speak without thinking may go back and forth on decisions and this confuses a Narrow Eyes Individual.

RECTANGULAR EYES

Rectangular Eyes are narrowed eyes that are *straight* on the top and bottom. Those with this eye shape take time contemplating their words before speaking. They speak from the head and don't let others in easily. In the jobs they accept, they tend to opt for security.

The world in which Rectangular Eyes Individuals live is not based on feelings. The straight lines suggest reason and levelheadedness. Rectangular Eyes Individuals have a gift for analysis, detail, and facts. They have the ability to concentrate on and investigate matters. These eyes are logical eyes for research, legal, and technical positions. Rectangular Eyes show intelligence when dealing with classified information. They bring many gifts but also the possible challenge of being cold.

Looking for a partner? On a first date with a Rectangular Eyes Individual don't talk about feelings; instead, converse about facts. Have confidence in what you have to say, because a Rectangular Eyes Individual can detect weakness and might want to debate. Be aware that exaggerations, generalizations, and misinformation may close your date's mind to the topic and to you. To gain trust, talk of things that are true.

There is an old saying that you can't fit a square peg into a round hole. And you can't make a Rectangular Eyes Individual respond as a person with Round Eyes would. A Round Eyes Individual might want his or her Rectangular Eyes partner to speak freely from the heart, the way he or she does. But it is not in a Rectangular Eyes Individual's nature to do so.

Color communicates too!

BROWN EYES

Brown Eyes reveal a serious nature. Brown Eyes indicate a person likely to make a good team player; these individuals are good at sharing. They are good at carrying out plans and when they direct their efforts to something in life, they apply themselves to it fully. They like to learn and are always interested in improving themselves.

A Brown Eyes Individual tends to spend lots of time thinking of those people who are close, or to matters in which he or she is closely involved. Family usually is very important, and the darker the brown, the more loyal the individual is said to be. Brown Eyes suggest down-to-earth sensitivity.

Eye color plays only a small part in defining a person's personality and this is especially true for Brown Eyes. The majority of people in the world have Brown Eyes. Each individual is unique, and when reading a face, remember not to assess character by considering only one feature or aspect of it.

BLUE EYES

Blue Eyes suggest a high level of self-confidence, emotional sensitivity, and truthfulness. Individuals with *light* Blue Eyes tend to be frank, opinionated, outspoken, and like to flirt. They are often bold individuals.

Dark Blue Eyes tell that carefully considered communication is very important; these individuals give more thought to the words they write or speak than those with eyes of lighter blue. *Dark* Blue Eyes suggest an individual who is more analytical than one with *light* Blue Eyes.

A *dark* Blue Eyes partner is likely to become distant when needing to protect his or her feelings. A *light* Blue Eyes partner is not likely to hesitate in telling you how he or she feels.

GREEN EYES

Green Eyes reveal an independent and self-sufficient individual with curiosity and a need to grow and expand. Green Eyes suggest a mysterious and a deeply emotional person. Green Eyes Individuals have a natural competitive streak and are prone to jealousy.

Green Eyes Individuals are very determined individuals who overcome obstacles and create opportunities. The color green also suggests a healing potential and a gift for money.

These individuals are stimulated by meeting and talking to new people and do it when they can. The Green Eyes Individual you are currently dating, however, is quite likely to become suspicious if he or she sees you talking to someone new.

BLUE-GREEN EYES

Blue-Green Eyes show that communication is important and reveal a gift for it. Clear Blue-Green Eyes have a soothing influence on others, which helps communication flow more easily. Restricting communication negatively impacts a Blue-Green Eyes Individual's wellbeing. When those with this eye color are not able to express themselves, energy becomes stuck and lighter shades of Blue-Green Eyes take on a grey appearance.

If a Blue-Green Eyes Individual leaves a message asking you to "please call back," not responding to this request in a timely manner is likely not to be taken lightly. A Blue-Green Eyes Individual has a stronger *need* to communicate than most.

HAZEL EYES

Hazel Eyes have a brown center surrounded by green. Flecks of red or gold may also be seen. Hazel Eyes are a mixture of colors and can change colors. Lighting, mood, and clothing have the ability to change the eyes' appearance.

Hazel Eyes suggest flexible, accommodating, broad-minded individuals who enjoy variety and are good at multitasking. This color reveals one who likes new experiences and is open to trying things. Hazel Eyes Individuals tend to be caring, considerate individuals who have a strong need to be liked.

A Hazel Eyes date may have an easy time fitting in to different social situations due his or her adaptable nature.

GREY EYES

Grey Eyes suggest reserved individuals. When it comes to dealing with others, they tend to be deep and somewhat secretive. Often they are shy people. They dislike confrontations and difficulties and do what they can to avoid them. There is refinement seen in Grey Eyes along with gifts for balance, logic, and reason.

A Grey Eyes partner may be more reasonable than passionate, but most often will be someone on whom you can depend.

BLACK EYES

Some eyes look black, but most are really a very dark brown. Black Eyes are rare and striking, indicating intelligence and insight, as well as an overactive mind and excitable nervous system. Black Eyes Individuals are persuasive and determined. They do not accept defeat easily. This trait can be beneficial for making sales in business, distinguishing oneself in sports, and achieving personal goals.

A Black Eyes Individual may be difficult to find, but if found might be difficult to live with.

THREE WHITES

The white part of an eye is the sclera and is usually only seen at the sides of an eye. When white shows above or below the iris, (the colored part of the eye), this may be called Three Whites. Three Whites tells of some sort of inner unrest.

White seen on the *bottom* (below the iris) reveals stress and depletion. *Bottom* Three Whites Individuals are likely to be living on nervous energy and reacting emotionally. A *Bottom* Three Whites Individual could be this way due to illness, depression, or adrenal depletion. These individuals are having trouble coping. Rest and rebalancing is needed.

When the white is on *top*, this type of Three Whites reveals a tightly wound nervous system. *Top* Three Whites Individuals have a startled

Bottom Three Whites

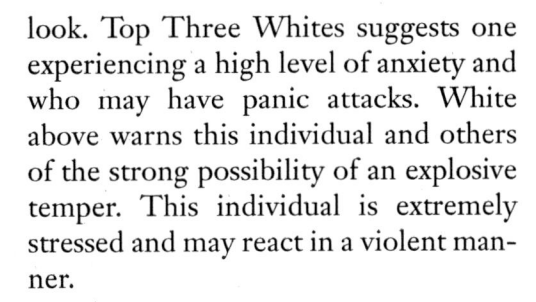

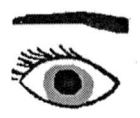

Top Three Whites

Four Whites

look. Top Three Whites suggests one experiencing a high level of anxiety and who may have panic attacks. White above warns this individual and others of the strong possibility of an explosive temper. This individual is extremely stressed and may react in a violent manner.

The gift of seeing Three Whites is that it reveals an imbalance. Becoming aware of this can enable a Three Whites Individual to attempt to do something about it. The gift for others is that once they learn the meaning behind the Three Whites, they can understand a Three Whites Individual better.

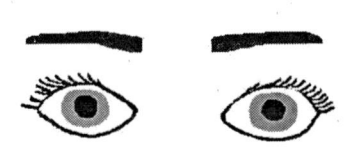

Those around a Three Whites Individual may wish to modify their words or actions. Three Whites Individuals tend to be edgy and hypersensitive and may easily feel attacked.

If your partner has *Bottom* Three Whites, he or she might look to you and others for reassurance. This is something these individuals tend to do.

FOUR WHITES

White seen on all four sides of the iris is known as Four Whites. Four Whites is very rare. Four Whites suggest one who is tense, has sharp reactions, and often a sharp mind. Four Whites can reveal a manic individual.

Four Whites Individuals tend to think in atypical ways and their minds often border on genius. When in control of their reactions, they can make good use of their talents and can be good at managing people. Unfortunately, however, they are not always in control.

Movement throws others off balance

SHIFTY EYES

Eyes that move quickly from side to side can throw others off balance. Shifty Eyes may be only a temporary condition, but if the eyes always shift, and are somewhat *narrowed*, this is a sign the individual may have something to hide. If you are single and seeking, perhaps it may be best to direct your sight to someone else. This individual might be lying to you. Shifty Eyes reveals the likelihood that the individual is untrustworthy, dishonest, or deceitful. But, this is not always the case.

Very honest people may also shift their eyes. They may lower their lids as well. Some people shift their eyes because it is part of their culture; they are taught it is not polite to stare. Others with Shifty Eyes are just introverted, nervous, and shy. They become more so when someone looks into their eyes. These Shifty Eyes Individuals tend to blush. They most often have nothing to hide but shift their eyes for protection. These individuals are quite hard on themselves and require patience and understanding. If you are this type of Shifty Eyes Individual, remove yourself from people and situations in which you don't feel safe.

If on a date with someone who seems very shy, rather than sitting across the table where you would look eye-to-eye, sit next to your date, side-by-side. But not too close.

THE TEMPLES

The temples are located on the sides of a forehead, between eyes and hairline. Temples can reveal if an individual is comfortable living in the present space and time or has a desire to be somewhere else. Temples can tell of a tendency for addiction or may reveal a very creative or very spiritual individual. The temples correspond to the Wood element.

A temple might be a holy place

Temples can be deeply indented. Temples may also be full or only slightly indented. The temples show *desire for altered states*.

FULL TEMPLES

When temples are not indented, they are Full Temples. They indicate a person who does not actively desire an altered state of mind. A Full Temples Individual might have an easier time living a simple life. Full Temples suggest one comfortable in his or her skin and one who might have an easier time being present in a relationship.

DEEPLY INDENTED TEMPLES

When temples are concave, forming a noticeable groove, they are Deeply Indented Temples. The bigger the indentation, the more the individual desires an altered state of mind. There are many reasons that a person could have Deeply Indented Temples.

Deeply Indented Temples Individuals tend to have an addictive personality. Some use drugs, alcohol, food, gambling, or sex to escape reality. Deeply Indented Temples can also show compulsive behavior or hyperactivity. This type of behavior can take countless forms; working too much is an example of a form this behavior might take.

When Deeply Indented Temples have an obvious *dark cast* to them, this suggests one who *habitually escapes* through addictive chemical substances or other forms of low vibration pleasure seeking. Violent pornography and dog fights carry a low vibration and watching such type of entertainment is an example of this. A person with Deeply Indented Temples *without a dark cast* might no longer escape through mood altering substances or "dark side" activities but may possibly have done so in the past.

Deeply Indented Temples can also reveal a *deeply spiritual* individual. Residing in a meditative state or adhering to a serious yoga practice might be a big part of this individual's life.

Individuals who are very *creative* often lose track of space and time when deeply involved in their work. They find pleasurable escape through their creativity. They, too, may be Deeply Indented Temples Individuals.

If your partner has Deeply Indented Temples and is on a serious spiritual path, he or she might have less and less interest in common pastimes such as playing games, attending sporting events, or watching television. Others may not understand, but if you are like-minded, you will.

When dating, it is important to know what works for you. Depending on your state of mind, a person who desires altered states may or may not be a great find.

THE NOSE

Interested in money? Look at the nose, for it is the area on the face representing career and wealth. The nose shows what motivates an individual, reveals work style, financial priorities, energy for work, and money management. The size of one's ego is suggested in the nose; support given and received is revealed as well. The nose corresponds to the Metal Element.

As an aside, lines that form next to the nostrils and go past the mouth are called nasolabial folds and are considered "good" lines according to Chinese face readers. They reveal one has found his or her life's purpose; a fortunate thing!

Size suggests the need to make a statement

As with other features, the size of a nose is judged in proportion to the size of a face. There is no exact measurement to determine nose size, but if it looks to be large or small, it likely is. Nose size reveals *the need to make an impact, especially in the area of work.*

LARGE NOSE

A Large Nose might come off a face or its base might spread wide across a face. A Large Nose suggests desire for recognition. Large Nose Individuals tend to be ambitious. This nose size reveals gifts for creating wealth and obtaining material success.

Long Nose

Short Nose

Large Nose

Small Nose

A Large Nose also shows an independent spirit and a need to make a major impact, especially through work. Many traits found in Large Nose Individuals are traits associated with successful business people. Being a worker among workers is not for Large Nose Individuals nor will they be content doing tedious tasks. A Large Nose indicates a desire to make a significant contribution and a need to be in charge at some level.

A Large Nose reveals force of character and a pushing forward of the personality. But those who push too hard to make an impact often don't have the most pleasing personality. Large Nose Individuals must be mindful of this.

Not all Large Nose Individuals come from a "material place," however. A Large Nose can tell of non-physical abundance. Large Nose Individuals might ask themselves "How can I make a difference in the world? How can I use my gifts to benefit others?"

You may have a Large Nose partner who has always wished for a nose not as big. You, too, may have secretly thought a smaller nose might be more attractive. If surgery to reduce the nose size is being considered, know that inherent power and gifts will be diminished.

Your partner with a Large Nose may be in need a job. Although you might be unhappy if he or she takes a long time getting one, your partner will be unhappy taking just any one. Understand a Large Nose Individual's nature.

SMALL NOSE

A nose is considered small when it is small compared with the size of the face. A Small Nose suggests an unassuming nature and less ego involvement concerning position or work. These individuals tend not to feel a strong need to make a major impact in the world.

Most often they do not have a big need to be noticed. There may be less ambition when it comes to career. Humility is a trait often found in Small Nose Individuals. When it comes to work, their focus is in the moment. They stick to the task at hand and get the job done. When a nose is small, but *not sharp*, this suggests a warm and loving personality.

If your partner has a Small Nose, he or she may be thoughtful, loyal, and dedicated, but may not be thought of as being powerful at work.

Length reveals planning time needed

When looking at the nose, the length can be determined by comparing it with size of the face. Nose length shows *length of planning time*.

LONG NOSE

A nose that is long in proportion to the face is a Long Nose. It shows farsighted cautiousness. Work is done with refinement, good sense, and forethought. This nose reveals a gift for planning. And, when it comes to planning, these individuals tend to take a long time.

When it comes to work, Long Nose Individuals need to be in control of their environment, the order, and the pace with which work gets done. It is important they are not rushed. Care is put into projects, and before moving forward, they desire a solid strategy be in place. The *quality* of their work output is more important to them than *quantity* of work put out.

Financially, a Long Nose suggests one who values tradition and security. Long Nose Individuals plan ahead for their wealth, preferring proven, controlled approaches.

A Long Nose partner will find it more important to do a job right than to do it quickly and is likely to need extra time. You might need extra patience waiting for your partner to start or to finish a particular project. However, the result will tend to be good.

SHORT NOSE

When a nose is short in proportion to the face, it is a Short Nose. A Short Nose reveals a hard worker who gets to the task at hand and gets the job done. Short Nose Individuals focus on what is in front of them at the moment.

They have a talent for figures and details and tend not to be bothered by repetition or routine. Short Nose Individuals are not at their best when it comes to planning and strategy; they often prefer projects be given to them.

Dedicated to service and commitment, Short Nose Individuals have a gift for production but the potential challenge of working too much. When it comes to work output, they feel that *quantity* is very important.

A Short Nose is also a sign of musical endowment. Powerful singers typically have a Short Nose and greater length in the lower portion of their face.

If you have a Long Nose and your partner has a Short Nose, it may work out best if you are in charge of long-range financial planning.

Your date might have a Short Nose. A Short Nose suggests one whose work is not driven by ego. Short Nose Individuals are motivated when they have lots of work that needs to get out quickly, and motivated when they love what they do. Because they require little planning time, they can accomplish a lot. Your Short Nose date might be an accomplished individual.

Protruding Nose

A protruding nose shows a pioneering personality

Some noses "come off the face" and others stick closer to it. Nose projection shows *independence and competitiveness*.

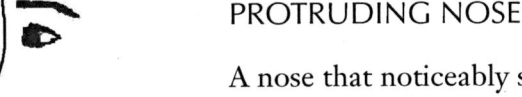

Flat Nose

PROTRUDING NOSE

A nose that noticeably sticks out from face is a Protruding Nose. It reveals a pioneering personality and adventurous spirit.

Protruding Nose Individuals are progressive in thoughts and actions. This nose brings a gift for introducing new and different ways to do things. Those with this nose are independent-minded individuals who stand out from crowds, live to move forward, and rebel at routine. Not followers, they tend not to be eager to join groups. They enjoy competition and like to prove themselves.

These spirited individuals can find success and excitement through work when what they do is revolutionary, groundbreaking, novel, or new. Protruding Nose Individuals are innovative trailblazers who need to make use of their gift.

Your Protruding Nose date might accompany you to a yoga class but may not be happy stuck in the middle with others, following along and doing the same old thing. Your date might (secretly) wish to be out in front leading others in poses no one has previously done because he or she just invented them.

FLAT NOSE

A nose that lies close to the face or is depressed in the center may be termed a Flat Nose. It brings a gift for working in harmony. Those with this nose tend to have a less competitive spirit. More than trying to outdo others, they are more apt to feel they can't do without others. They have an easier time seeing the interconnected nature of all life.

This nose is a sign of a valuable team player. (An exception to this is when a Flat Nose is *large*, for this indicates a person who needs to be in charge.) Most often, Flat Nose Individuals enjoy working where there is a common purpose and where information is shared.

Flat Nose Individuals are social people. Friends and family have high priority in their lives. More focused on connections than being independent in spirit, where travel is concerned, you may find them in groups.

You may have a Large Nose that stands out and a partner with a Flat Nose that blends in. Your idea of success might likely differ from that of your partner. Success doesn't always mean having the world take notice. One can achieve much by realizing his or her gifts and making good use of them.

Work style is shown in the shape

When viewed in profile, noses come in three basic shapes: straight, arched, and concave. Many have no distinct shape and are a blending of shapes. Nose shape tells of *work style*.

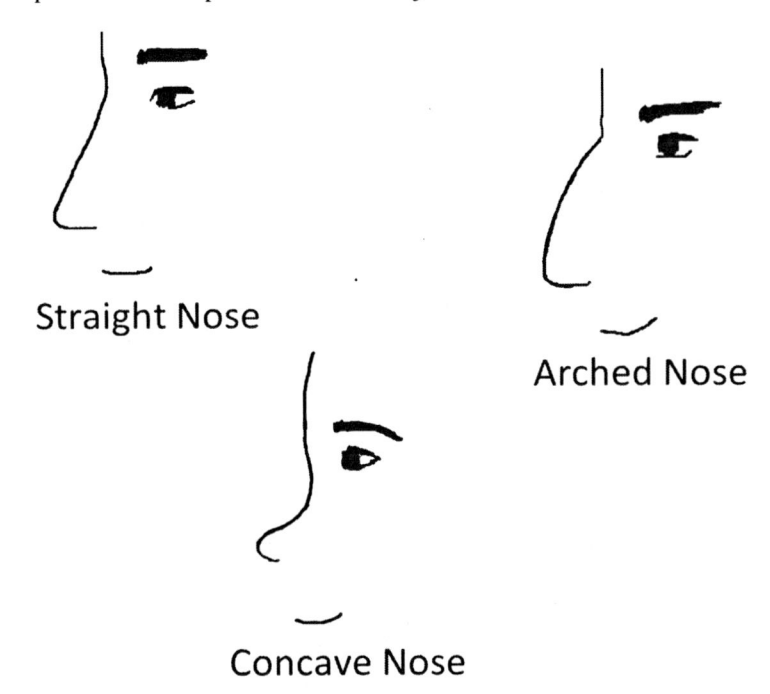

Straight Nose

Arched Nose

Concave Nose

STRAIGHT NOSE

When the spine of the nose is in a straight line, it is a Straight Nose. It tells of a straightforward style when it comes to work. These individuals like following proven plans and procedures. When setting goals they prefer a direct path.

A Straight Nose shows a balanced and logical approach. These individuals like checklists and working systematically. Working this way maintains focus and keeps them on track; it enhances their ability to reach goals and complete tasks. To them, their work style is just common sense. Self-will is also revealed in a Straight Nose, but not the aggressive type that is found in an Arched Nose.

Straight Nose Individuals tend to be respected for their sound judgment and practical ways; most often, they show respect for others.

They get to the point when dealing with others. Most can be counted on as being honest, stable, and trustworthy.

If your partner has a Straight Nose, he or she is likely to be straight and upfront with you, although you may not always want to hear his or her frank opinion. Be prepared when you ask how you look.

ARCHED NOSE

When the nose curves out, it is a convex nose. It can also be termed an Arched Nose. Arched Nose Individuals have a creative style of working, a pioneering disposition, and an adventurous spirit. This nose brings a talent for solving problems in innovative ways. These individuals appreciate beauty and elegance. Some have extravagant taste.

An Arched Nose indicates a strong self-will and a need to be out front and in charge. Many have a gift for leadership. They like challenges in the work they do as it brings out their creativity and energizes them. They delight in outdoing themselves and others. To make use of their gifts and talents, Arched Nose Individuals need a sense of freedom.

In situations with too many rules, policies, and procedures, they can feel stifled and frustrated. Due to the natural need to do things their way, some Arched Nose Individual become mentally aggressive in their attempt to have their way. An individual with this nose is not made for service positions.

The Arched Nose shows a gift for managing people, projects, and money. This nose suggests a strong desire for money, which brings a talent for making it. Entrepreneurs, politicians, business executives, and those working in finance might benefit from having an Arched Nose.

A partner with an Arched Nose will want to be the boss.

CONCAVE NOSE

When a nose is curved in when viewed from profile, it is a Concave Nose. Concave Nose Individuals have a "people approach" style of working and a gift for uplifting others. Traits associated with this nose can be advantageous in social situations. These individuals have a talent for helping others feel good. They tend not to seek power through their work but may work as assistants to those seeking it. A Concave Nose shows a gift for being of service.

A Concave Nose suggests a friendly, caring nature. Emotions impact the work of these individuals, and they are most productive working in a supportive environment where they are appreciated and acknowledged for their efforts. They tend to trust easily, which can sometimes be a challenge.

A Concave Nose suggests one whose work is not motivated by money. Some find it difficult to charge for work they do. Concave Nose Individuals are drawn to service-oriented careers; indeed, many work as volunteers. They don't do their best in an isolated environment or being in business for themselves. They tend to be generous with affection and may be generous in other ways as well. They are happiest when being of assistance. They thrive when being able to serve.

A Concave Nose Individual may or may not be an evolved soul, but evolved souls do tend to be generous, helpful, and friendly; traits that are associated with the Concave Nose.

If your partner has a Concave Nose, he or she may get pleasure from encouraging, giving, and caring for others. Perhaps you feel you are not as giving. Give appreciation; it will be appreciated.

When a person with a nose that naturally curves out changes it through surgery to a nose that curves in, don't be surprised if as a result he or she feels a bit confused.

Energy for work is found across the bridge

The nose bridge is the upper, boney part of the nose. Width is determined subjectively. If a nose bridge looks wide or narrow, it probably is.

A horizontal line across a nose bridge suggests burnout and reveals a person who has been pushing him- or herself too hard and is likely to be exhausted. Those with these lines tend to be very responsible individuals. The nose bridge width shows both *energy and focus for work.*

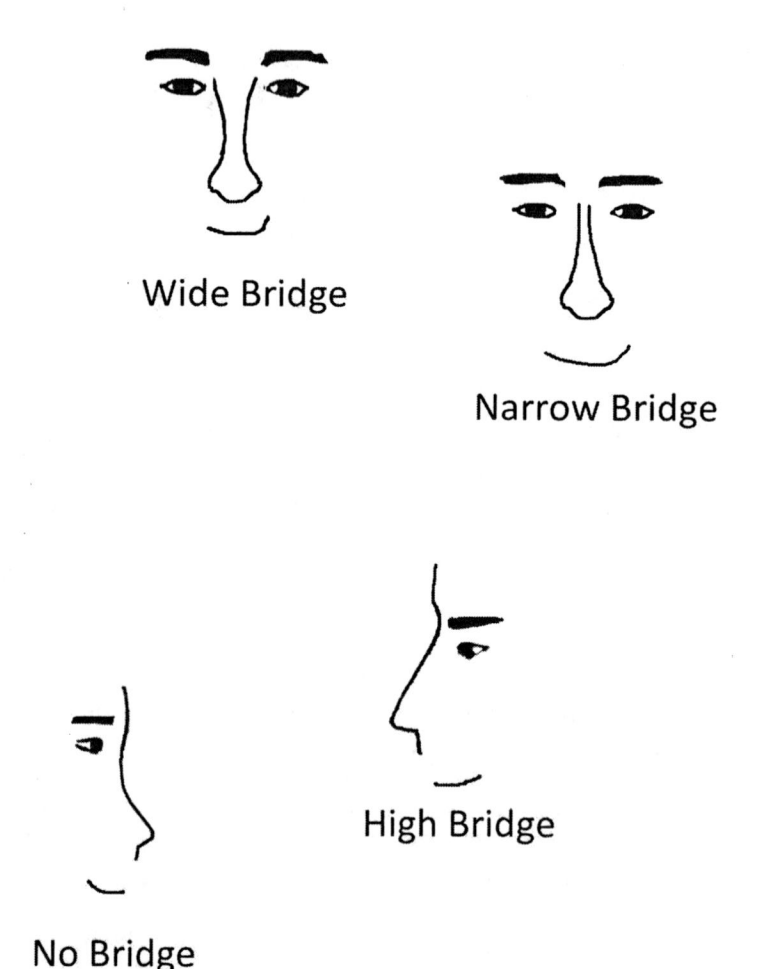

Wide Bridge

Narrow Bridge

High Bridge

No Bridge

WIDE BRIDGE

A Wide Bridge reveals strength and an abundance of energy for work. It also tells of a broad focus. These individuals have a gift for bringing in money from many different sources. Concerning work, Wide Bridge Individuals have a wide range of opportunities.

Wide Bridge Individuals go after what they want; they are determined and work hard to make money. And, Wide Bridge Individuals may need to make a lot of money; most are quite fond of material things.

A Wide Bridge reveals significant room for ideas and a talent for handling several things simultaneously. The ability to manage multiple businesses or multiple streams of income can help in multiplying money. However, too many varied interests might lead to a lack of focus, which hampers the ability to succeed in any single endeavor.

When a Wide Bridge is *high*, this suggests one who works best independently. Career is likely to take priority in this individual's life. When a Wide Bridge is *low*, this suggests one oriented toward family. A family-run business might be where this individual succeeds.

A Wide Bridge that *bulges at the sides* reveals a feisty individual. A person with this type of bridge should not work in a position in which he or she feels trapped. This person needs a sense of freedom in relationships as well.

If you are in a confined work space with an individual with a Wide Bridge that *bulges at the sides*, it may not be possible to keep out of his or her way. Avoid confrontations if you can.

You notice your date has a line across the nose bridge that you learned (from this book) suggests exhaustion. But, before you become concerned, concerning your date, there is another possible reason for this. A horizontal line across the bridge can also appear if a person wears eyeglasses and has just taken them off.

NARROW BRIDGE

A Narrow Bridge reveals focused energy when it comes to work. These Individuals do best when concentrating on one type of work at a time. A Narrow Bridge brings the gift of a clear direction in life; a clear focus brings in more than enough money.

A Narrow Bridge shows perfectionist tendencies. Precision and quality tend to be very important to those with a Narrow Bridge. They excel at work that requires exactness and attention to detail. When used wisely, their gift can bring much success. Obsession with perfection however, can get in the way of completing projects or moving forward in life. A Narrow Bridge suggests some difficulty letting go of thoughts and the potential to judge others harshly.

If your partner has a very Narrow Bridge, he or she may hold on to things that you said or did that you wish to be forgotten. Your partner may hold on even more if you call these concerns "little things." You can't change your partner, but you can refuse to participate in a repetitious conversation. A partner with this challenge might at times *be* a challenge, but keep in mind this challenge is likely difficult for him or her.

If dating a Narrow Bridge Individual, you may find this person feels that the correct use of words is very important.

A high level of self-will is seen in a High Bridge

The nose bridge can be high, low, or somewhere in between. Some bridges are flat and not even seen. Nose bridge height reveals *self-will*.

HIGH BRIDGE

When a nose bridge is high, close to the level of the brows, it is a High Bridge. A High Bridge makes a nose more prominent and suggests one who is confident, determined, and opinionated. These individuals tend to be self-willed and work best independently.

High Bridge Individuals have an enhanced ability to draw attention to their talents and excel when using their gifts in their work. This nose tells of strong drive and ambition; High Bridge Individuals become frustrated in situations in which they are held back.

High Bridge Individuals are most often very sure of their abilities and want to do what they want to do. A challenge for those with a High Bridge is to take care not to be unteachable, insensitive, or selfish.

A partner with a High Bridge is likely to respond very negatively to being told what to do. If you would like your partner to do something, use care in wording your request. Actually, this is the way to treat all people.

LOW OR NO BRIDGE

When the nose bridge is flat or low, the bridge may be termed a Low or No Bridge. When it comes to work, it suggests one who enjoys working with others in an environment where knowledge and experiences are shared. A Low or No Bridge reveals a gift for teamwork; these individuals tend to feel lonely when working alone.

A Low or No Bridge suggests less self-will, making these individuals easier to get along with. They typically don't push to have things their way nor do they tend to seek to be in charge. Valued for their flexibility and cooperation at work, they place high value on co-workers and friends.

The ability to control and direct is not what makes a great leader. Great leaders are those who show respect for people and their work. If your partner with a Low or No Bridge is promoted to a management or leadership position, the gift for working well with others can bring support from others. This, in turn, can help your partner lead.

Bumps reveal a spirited individual

Boney bumps may be found on a nose bridge or may be seen along the length of the spine of a nose. No matter where a bump appears, it tells of a need to be in charge. Boney nose bumps reveal *force of will*.

BRIDGE BUMP

When a boney bump is on a nose bridge, it is a Bridge Bump. A Bridge Bump reveals a spirited individual. Bridge Bump Individuals are proud, determined, and are likely to become feisty when they feel trapped. They work best independently. They have the gift of a strong drive when it comes to work and when they follow their life's purpose they can become very successful.

A Bridge Bump tells of a fighting spirit. This can be advantageous in certain business situations, such as when an attorney argues for a client. In particular personal matters, it is often found useful. Bridge Bump Individuals don't give up and won't let others down. And, they won't let others put them down. A fighting spirit, used wisely, is a gift.

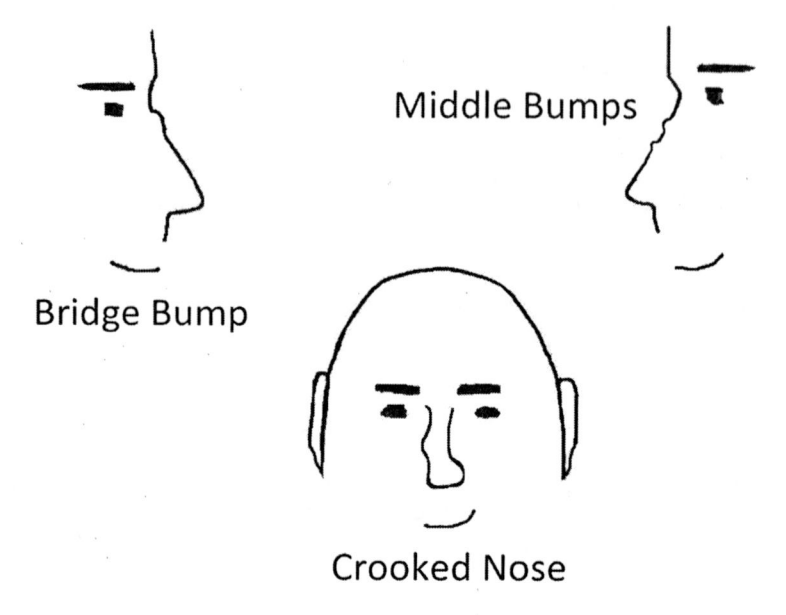

Middle Bumps

Bridge Bump

Crooked Nose

Potential challenges can arise for Bridge Bump Individuals when they need to relinquish control and work as a team player. Most are not the happiest stay-at-home moms or dads although they can do this for a short period of time. These are rebellious individuals who push against restrictions and rebel at rules. They are not at their best working in service positions. It may be better for them and others if they don't.

If your partner has a Bridge Bump you may wish to concede in matters that are not that important. Not everything is worth fighting for.

MIDDLE BUMP(S)

One bump in the middle of the length of a nose is a Middle Bump. Nose bumps in general suggest a person who works best independently. Originality may be found in a Middle Bump Individual's work.

Team projects can be tough; cooperating with others is often a challenge.

Two or more bumps down the length of a nose are Middle Bumps. Middle Bumps suggest a unique sense of inner timing, and those who don't take logical approaches when it comes to work. These are willful individuals whose enthusiasm comes in spurts. Middle Bumps reveal spontaneity, originality, and courage. Freedom of expression is very important to them. When a bump bulges at the sides it reveals a feisty individual.

Middle Bumps can reveal a powerful individual who is holding back opinions and talents. Middle Bumps can also tell of sudden starts and stops in midlife career. The spine of the nose also corresponds to the spine of an individual and bumps sometimes indicate problems with a person's back.

If you have just started dating someone with Middle Bumps, he or she may at times do things in ways that don't seem to make *sense*. But, when it comes to *cents*, his or her financial picture may have straightened out. This is particularly true if he or she is over 50. (On the Chinese age map the nose corresponds to one's 40s.)

Desire to save may be seen in the tip

The end of a nose is the nose tip. It may be full and fleshy or boney, thin, or pointed. As with all features, many fall in the midrange. A groove in the tip indicates a person's heart is not in his or her work. This person may be doing a job just for the money. The nose tip tells of *interest in financial security*.

CHUNKY TIP

When the end of the nose is full and fleshy, it is a Chunky Tip. The bigger the tip the greater the concern one has with money. Financial security tends to be very important to Chunky Tip individuals.

A Chunky Tip doesn't mean one *has* a lot of money, but it does suggest one has a great deal of interest in *accumulating* it. Those who have saving as a priority have an easier time putting money away. A Chunky Tip suggests one who enjoys pleasures of the material world and can reveal a connoisseur of food.

A Chunky Tip also shows interest in accumulating things. Some have a Chunky Tip in the shape of a ball. When a *big ball* is found at the end of the nose, this suggests a collector of some sort. When a Chunky Tip is in the shape of a *small ball*, this suggests artistic gifts and appreciation of beauty.

If the end of the nose appears *puffy*, however, this indicates some type of stagnation. A *puffy* nose suggests a need for circulation and can indicate a one's heart may be more closed than open.

There are those with Chunky Tips and lots of money who live as if they have no money. Some millionaires are found to fret about finances, buy few clothes, and drive old cars. Doing this may or may not make them happy, but it is their nature and is what they do. If dating an individual like this, remember this if you think he or she might change. Look, too, at the nose holes to discover more about spending and saving habits. Read on, to learn about nostrils.

On a side note: In modern Western culture prosperity tends to be thought of in terms of money. In old Chinese culture, a person was considered *prosperous* in old age when he or she had an *abundance* of children and grandchildren who lived close by.

THIN TIP

A nose tip with more bone than padding is a Thin Tip. A Thin Tip suggests saving money and accumulating possessions is not a priority. Some Thin Tip Individuals inherited wealth and don't have financial concerns. Others just don't have financial concerns. The bonier the tip, the less interest one has in planning for security. Thin Tip Individuals may be interested in money, but this nose suggests more interest in spending than saving.

Some Thin Tip Individuals are more spiritually than materially minded and spend wisely without worry or fear. They feel no need to save or accumulate. When a need appears, what is needed appears.

A *very boney nose with a boney* Thin Tip might reveal an attraction to a hard life, often for deep reasons the individual might not fully understand. Others might not understand this attraction to hardship. What is important for others to understand, however, is not the hardship attraction, but that people are unique and don't have the same values or think the same way. *A very boney nose with a boney* Thin Tip can also be a sign of a strong individual.

You may have a Thin Tip along with a bank balance on the thin side. If you are single and seeking, perhaps you think a full, fleshy, chunky tipped individual might help you get control of your finances. Spendthrifts often seek tightwads. However, a relationship such as this could be challenging, for those who like to spend and those who like to save don't always see eye to eye. If seeking a lasting love match, consider this tip.

You might be concerned that your Thin Tip partner is not saving money. Some people take their focus off acquiring assets knowing that prosperity and abundance can grow when the focus is on giving.

The nose tip direction points out one's point of view

A nose tip might point up or down. Many have no angle, suggesting a balance of extremes. Nose tip direction tells of *trust in others*.

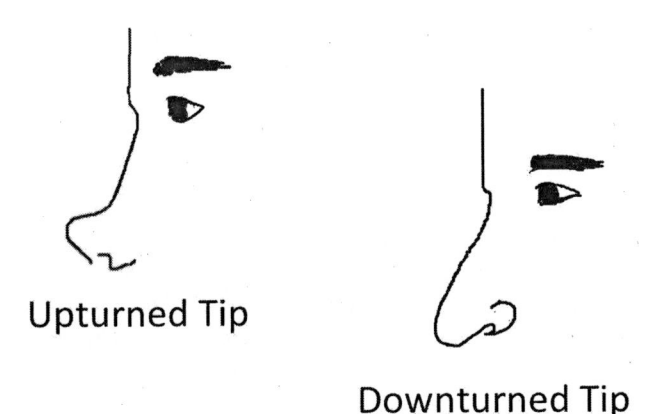

Upturned Tip

Downturned Tip

UPTURNED TIP

When the nose tip points up, it is an Upturned Tip. It reveals an optimistic point of view and cheery attitude. Upturned Tip Individuals tend to trust others easily.

An Upturned Tip suggests a spontaneous, enthusiastic approach to life. These individuals have an easier time than those with a Downturned Tip when it comes to believing what people say. They like fun, are likely to fall into relationships quickly, and may fall for get-rich-quick schemes. An Upturned Tip tells of a childlike nature, which can be both a challenge and a gift.

This tip can bring impulsive tendencies leading to challenges focusing on work or completing tasks. These individuals live in the moment and may *feel* more than they *think*. An Upturned Tip suggests a carefree approach to spending.

If your partner's nose tip points up, and the tip is *pointed*, your partner is likely to have intense curiosity, especially when it comes to hearing about others. A pointed Upturned Tip also brings interest in hearing the details of issues and situations.

DOWNTURNED TIP

When a nose tip points down, it is a Downturned Tip. A Downturned Tip reveals a skeptical nature. These individuals need proof before believing something to be true. A Downturned Tip suggests it will take time for this individual to trust someone.

The gift of a Downturned Tip is the good level of common sense these individuals tend to have. They take a deliberate and logical approach and this can bring success when it comes to career. However, a Downturned Tip Individual might need to guard against coming across as selfish when making decisions. And, there is the potential challenge of being cold in the pursuit of ambition.

When the tip points down excessively, this suggests a firm handle on managing money. A Downturned Tip also tells of a talent for sensing unscrupulous salespeople. These gifts can help these individuals hold on to money even more.

A Downturned Tip partner might crush your enthusiasm by giving you an automatic "thumbs down" when you present a new idea. Perhaps your partner knows best at times. Other times, facts, proof, and substantiation are needed to persuade.

People can be attracted to one another due to a *subtle* smell that most individuals cannot detect. This is nature's way of attracting couples in their reproductive years. If you are dating, you may not understand your attraction to certain people. Scent might play a part in this mystery. A Downturned Tip can reveal a heightened sense of smell.

CROOKED NOSE

When viewing a nose from the front, if it points to the side, it is a Crooked Nose. A Crooked Nose might appear to be twisted.

The spine of a nose corresponds to the spine of the back and a Crooked Nose might reveal a back problem of some sort. This nose also suggests an individual who may not always be straight in business dealings. Strength of character might be needed to avoid deviating from what is right. These Crooked Nose Individuals trust others to the degree they trust themselves.

If you have a nose pointing to the left or right, this does not mean you are not honest and ethical. Nevertheless, it can point out one of your potential challenges.

If dating or in a relationship with a Crooked Nose Individual, remember that face reading shows tendencies and not absolutes. An individual with a Crooked Nose can be as honorable and principled as anyone else. And, the nose may just be crooked due to a back problem, the result a fight, or a botched nose job.

The bigger the holes, the more money flows

Nostrils come in different sizes and shapes. On some people, nostrils are difficult to see; on others you can see into them easily. Nostril size is determined subjectively. Nostrils circulate air through the lungs.

The larger the holes, the more vitality and endurance an individual will tend to have. Nostrils reveal *flow of energy and money*.

LARGE NOSTRILS

Large Nostrils reveal an expansive approach to life and Individuals who have an abundance of vitality and physical endurance.

Large Nostrils also suggest an open channel of money. Those with Large Nostrils tend to have an easier time spending money than those with nostrils that are small. The rounder the holes, the more one enjoys circulating money. Some Large Nostrils Individuals have a challenge when it comes to saving it.

HUGE FLARED NOSTRILS

When nostrils are very large and widen at the sides, they are Huge Flared Nostrils. They reveal an expansive approach to life and an individual with self-confidence, determination, and courage. An unrestricted flow of money is suggested by Huge Flared Nostrils. Intense energy is revealed.

Huge Flared Nostrils suggest an individual who lives life to the fullest. These Nostrils are found on extravagant spenders who buy the best. At times, however, they might overestimate their resources or abilities. Huge Flared Nostrils can indicate a big ego and an individual who needs to be in charge. Impatience is a possible challenge.

A partner with Huge Flared Nostrils likely has so much to do because he or she likes to do so much and has the energy for it.

LONG NARROW NOSTRILS

Skinny, long nostrils are Long Narrow Nostrils. They suggest a reduced level of stamina and endurance. Energy is best spent thoughtfully so as not to burn out.

Concerning finances, Long Narrow Nostrils reveal careful spending of money. These individuals take a conservative approach, and appreciate value. You'll likely find them looking for bargains.

Long Narrow Nostrils also tell of emotional generosity. Long Narrow Nostrils Individuals tend to get pleasure from the opportunity to give emotional support. Their gift is in giving of themselves. Long Narrow Nostrils suggest a less showy way of living than suggested in wider nose holes. Energy may be spent on intellectual matters or spiritual things.

SMALL NOSTRILS

When nostrils are both short and narrow, they are Small Nostrils. They suggest a tight hold on money. Small Nostrils Individuals tend to use restraint when it comes to spending. Focused thought is put into where their money goes.

Small Nostrils indicate the ability to save. Holding on to money tends to be a priority. They are less likely to fall for scams or give in to pressure from salespeople. But, Small Nostrils can sometimes disclose a perception of lack or fear of poverty. Small Nostrils in the shape of a triangle suggests a penny pincher.

Small Nostrils show some restriction in the ability to take in air and this reduces vitality and endurance; these individuals need to spend their energy wisely.

If your partner has a *large fleshy Chunky Tip* as well as *Small Nostrils*, money is likely spent wisely, and financial security probably is very important. Disagreements might arise if your purchases are frivolous or your spending is too carefree.

EXPOSED NOSTRILS

When it is easy to see into one's nostrils, the nostrils are Exposed Nostrils. Exposed Nostrils can reveal an individual who needs to be more cautious in regards to spending habits, *or* it may tell of a consciousness of abundance, prosperity, and wealth.

Exposed Nostrils are often seen on carefree spenders who find saving challenging. These nostrils are said to indicate a leakage of money. Individuals with Exposed Nostrils may need to be more conscious of their finances.

Exposed Nostrils can also be viewed energetically as an open channel and lack of stagnation. Exposed Nostrils Individuals with an elevated consciousness allow money to flow in and out freely. They know circulating abundance is important and that the true source of wealth is within and infinite.

To help determine if an Exposed Nostrils Individual needs to be more conscious of money, *or* if he or she has an *elevated consciousness* of money, ask yourself: "Does he or she ask for money?" and "Are his or her financial obligations being met?"

Nose wings show protection and support

On the outer and lower side of nostrils are nose wings. Nose wings cover nostrils and give width to the bottom of a nose. Nose wings suggest *ease of support given and received*.

Wide Wings

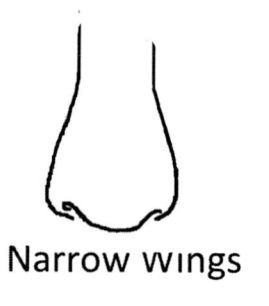

Narrow wings

WIDE WINGS

When a nose base extends widely to the sides, the nose has Wide Wings. Wide Wings show a wide base of generosity, protection, and support. These individuals are available to those close to them. They easily give and receive. Family, extended family, and friends who are like family are an important part of their lives.

When Wide Wings cover *large flared nostrils*, this reveals a very strong desire to provide for others. When Wide Wings are *thick* this reveals great potential for these individuals to be the superior providers they desire to be.

A Wide Wings partner will typically not hesitate to provide help to family and close friends when it is needed. One with Wide Wings might seem like an angel at times. You may feel supported with a partner with Wide Wings. But one with Wide Wings is likely to divide his or her time among multiple people and things. Being aware of a Wide Wing Individual's nature might help you avoid taking what seems like a lack of attention personally.

When considering a relationship, it is important that you know who you are, what you are looking for, and what you need. A person with a Wide Wings tends not to be an independent type or one who will be able to focus on you as much as you might like.

NARROW WINGS

When the nose wings don't extend out, but stick close to the side of the nose, they are Narrow Wings. Narrow Wings reveal self-reliant independent individuals and suggest one who may have trouble giving and receiving support. Many of these individuals grew up not properly nurtured and learned to depend on themselves. Narrow Wings often reveal a strong individual. Narrow Wings bring the gift of self-sufficiency and help one find his or her own direction in life.

Narrow Wings also reveal that this individual will tend to have more success making money when sticking to only one thing at a time.

An individual with Narrow Wings often has challenges in receiving from others. When dating a Narrow Wing Individual, he or she might resist if you give too much too soon.

THE PHILTRUM and the UPPER LIP AREA

The philtrum is the groove running between the nose and the mouth. A defined philtrum has strong vertical ridges. The philtrum tells of the need to create; fertility and desire for children may be reveled here. The philtrum corresponds to the Water element.

The groove gives clues to how one might want to be seen

On some individuals, a philtrum is deep; on others, it is barely perceivable. A philtrum may be long or short, wide or narrow. Philtrum depth suggests *fertility*.

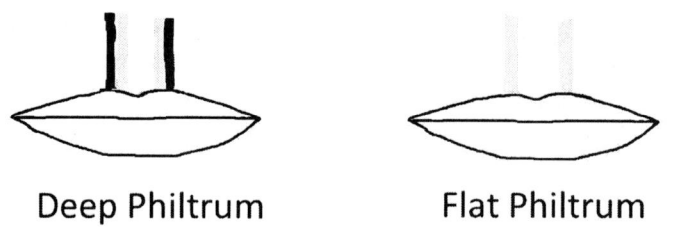

Deep Philtrum   Flat Philtrum

DEEP PHILTRUM

A deep groove between the nose and the area above the mouth is a Deep Philtrum. A Deep Philtrum suggests a strong reproductive system and fertility. It is nature's way of drawing attention to this.

When the lines are strongly *defined* this suggest one who tends to see the world in strongly defined male and female roles. A *wide* Deep

Philtrum shows a robust desire for sex, and a *long* Deep Philtrum suggests an intense desire for children. The *wider the base*, the more promise for productivity according to Chinese face reading.

If your date has a moustache, you will not be able to see if he might have a strong desire for children or enhanced fertility. Talking can answer the first question but not the second.

UNDEFINED PHILTRUM

A missing, flat, or barely perceivable philtium is an Undefined Philtrum. This suggests a lower level of fertility or can tell of less desire for children. These individuals can create in others ways. Ancient Taoists believed that it is easier for one to become spiritual when there is not a strong biological urge to reproduce.

Undefined Philtrum Individuals often wish to be valued for their intelligence, accomplishments, inner strength, or inner beauty more than for their sex appeal. Some might deliberately downplay their appearance.

You may be sexually interested in an Undefined Philtrum Individual or attracted to his or her look. Look deeper. There is more to him or her.

A long space suggests high self-esteem

As noted, the philtrum occupies the space between the base of the nose and the top of the lip. The *space* it occupies is termed the Upper Lip. The length of an Upper Lip suggests the level of *self-esteem*.

LONG UPPER LIP

When the nose-to-lip distance is long, it is a Long Upper Lip. A Long Upper Lip suggests an independent-minded individual with a high level of self-esteem.

A Long Upper Lip tells of confidence and self-assurance; Long Upper Lip Individuals may not care much about what others think. They

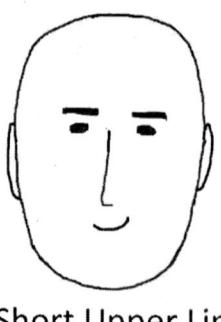

Short Upper Lip   **Long Upper Lip**

know who they are and are on guard for those who misrepresent themselves. They make up their own mind. When it comes to what they wear, they wear what *they* like. Long Upper Lip Individuals tend not to concern themselves with fashion trends. These individuals are okay with constructive criticism, but are not particularly gracious when someone gives them a piece of advice.

Long Upper Lip Individuals can often tell if someone is lying in an attempt to impress. They are skeptical by nature. Be sincere when giving your Long Upper Lip partner a compliment.

Long Upper Lip Individuals are known to have a dry sense of humor. If you are unaware of this, your feelings might get hurt if you don't see the humor in a Long Upper Lip date's remarks.

SHORT UPPER LIP

A short nose-to-lip distance is a Short Upper Lip. These individuals need approval. They value what others think of them and tend to give much thought to their looks. They often take criticism personally. Their attention to etiquette, however, can benefit them in social situations.

Some view a Short Upper Lip as desirable when it comes to appearance; in fact, it is found on Greek statues portraying beauty. A Short Upper Lip suggests one who places importance on appearance; these individuals tend to strive to look good. A Short Upper Lip, however, also indicates the potential challenge of *low self-esteem*.

Take care when joking around with your Short Upper Lip partner or date. A Short Upper Lip reveals one who does not like being teased.

THE MOUTH

The mouth reveals expressive potential and how an individual interprets what is being expressed. The mouth suggests a person's general outlook and indicates the importance one places on family and friends.

A mouth gives width and the lips provide fullness. Lips have meaning and are discussed in the next chapter. Both the mouth and lips correspond to the Earth element.

The width of the mouth whispers or shouts

A mouth's width is its horizontal measurement. The size is determined subjectively. Mouth width reveals the *size of audience* to which one is comfortable talking.

WIDE MOUTH

A Wide Mouth has a long width. It reveals comfort in talking to a large audience and reveals a gift for public speaking. Individuals with this mouth express confidence easily. They are happiest when are able to talk to many people and excel in situations in which they can do so. Wide Mouth Individuals find it challenging when talking is restricted.

Thin Lips on a Wide Mouth tell that good judgment and discretion will be used when talking business; this mouth brings a gift for confidentiality. These individuals are slower getting started when giving presentations but once started, pick up speed.

Wide Mouth

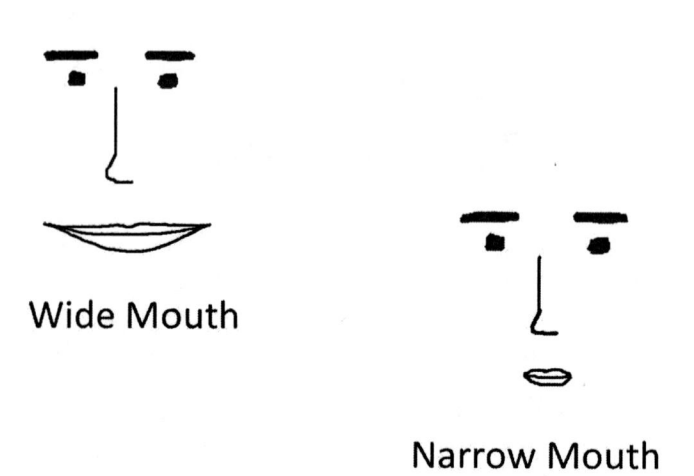

Narrow Mouth

Upturned Mouth

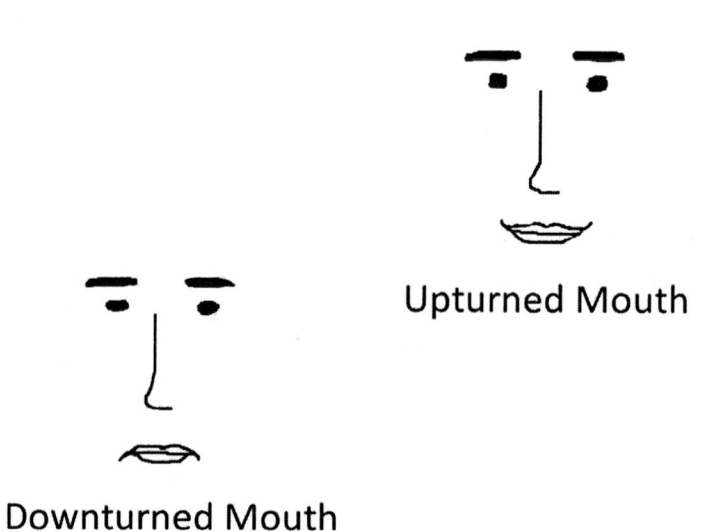

Downturned Mouth

Full Lips on a Wide Mouth brings a social advantage and reveals those likely to have many friends. *Full Lips* on a Wide Mouth reveals also a gift for singing and suggests comfort performing in front of large groups, but, less comfort conversing intimately.

A Wide Mouth on a *Broad Face* reveals the confidence to give a talk on the spot. A Wide Mouth on a *Narrow Face* suggests more preparation time will be needed before giving a talk.

A partner with a Wide Mouth will likely enjoy talking to many people. What is talked about may be revealed in the lips. See chapter following for more on this.

Close family connections are very important to those with a Wide Mouth and *Full Lips*. To be happy, they require lots of time with family, extended family, and friends who are like family. If you have just started dating someone with this type of mouth, you may view this as a challenge or a gift.

NARROW MOUTH

A Narrow Mouth has a short horizontal width. The lips may be full, thin, or somewhere in between.

Narrow Mouths reveal people who are most comfortable limiting the number of people to whom they talk at a time. They shy away from talking to groups and tend to be somewhat reserved in social situations. *Thin Lips* suggest one who is even more reserved.

Although one with a Narrow Mouth might talk to a very large audience through the medium of television, in front of the camera he or she might only be talking to one. A Narrow Mouth Individual may excel as an interviewer; this mouth shows the ability to gain trust easily. What others disclose to this person could be very revealing.

A gift of the Narrow Mouth is found in the sincerity of the words spoken. Strong emotions may be expressed only to those who are close.

Individuals with Narrow Mouths do not express their thoughts to just anyone. What your Narrow Mouth partner tells you is likely heartfelt and genuine.

For expectations of things turning out, look at the turn of the mouth

Mouth corners may turn up or down. Some do not turn but are straight. On some people, the corners don't match. When mouth corners are different, remember that the right side is the public side and the left side is the private side. The direction the mouth corners reveal how an individual *interprets what is being expressed.*

UPTURNED MOUTH

When the corners turn up, it is an Upturned Mouth. This mouth reveals an "up" attitude and outlook. An Upturned Mouth Individual sees the good in people, situations, and things. Many are drawn to Upturned Mouth Individuals, whereas some are annoyed by their cheerfulness. Those who are turned off tend to be those with mouths that turn down.

An Upturned Mouth suggests a trusting view of life and individuals who trust others. They interpret what is being expressed as positive; they trust others' words before mistrusting. An Upturned Mouth becomes rarer with age, as unhappy experiences set in and turn the mouth down. As such, an Upturned Mouth gives a youthful appearance; a gift for those with an Upturned Mouth.

If you have an Upturned Mouth, you likely have an optimistic outlook most of the time. A partner going through a difficult time may be irritated by your happiness and helpful suggestions. If so, acknowledge where your partner is and do some straight listening. Listening is a loving act and can be uplifting.

DOWNTURNED MOUTH

When the mouth's corners turn down, it is a Downturned Mouth. This mouth reveals a skeptical nature. These individuals may have difficulty hearing kindness and compliments; they are inclined to mistrust the motive. Downturned Mouth Individuals view life from the negative side first and are accustomed to things *not* working out. These individuals tend not to be phony. They are realists.

Downturned Mouth Individuals might complain or have negative things to say more often than most, but they don't speak without purpose or reason. Consider what a Downturned Mouth partner says. There may be some real truth to it.

A Downturned Mouth date needs to know you can be trusted before he or she will trust you. Don't take his or her nature personally.

This mouth reveals to a Downturned Mouth Individual, and to others, a tendency to be pessimistic. Awareness is the first step in motivating one to change. Not everyone, however, wants to.

THE LIPS

The lips relate to communication, appetite, and the enjoyment of sensual pleasures. Ease of expressing feelings and the ability to nurture oneself is revealed. Lips can become fuller when one is living a happier life. Lips correspond to the Earth element.

Expressiveness is found in the fullness

Lips vary in fullness. The fleshier the face, the fuller the lips will tend to be. Faces that are taut with delicate features tend to have naturally thinner lips. The top is normally the smaller of the two. The top and bottom have different meanings. Lip fullness reveals the amount of *comfort in verbal expression*.

FULL LIPS

Plump, fleshy, or thick lips are Full Lips. They reveal a gift for verbal expression. The fuller the lips, the more expressive an individual will be. Full Lips suggest one who is sensual and affectionate but *artificially* Full Lips disclose that the sensuality may not be real. Artificially Full Lips make known how the person wishes to be seen. This means both physically and emotionally.

Full Lips Individuals are comfortable communicating verbally. When Full Lips are *strong and thick* they reveal a forceful communicator who might be misunderstood by very sensitive people. This individual may come across as angry but may not really be. When Full Lips are *plump and soft*, words tend to come out with more tact and diplomacy.

Full Lips on a Wide Mouth

Thin Lips on a Narrow Mouth

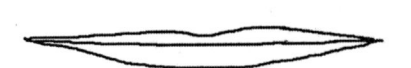

Thin Lips on a Wide Mouth

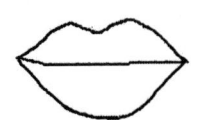

Full Lips on a Narrow Mouth

When Full Lips are on a *Wide Mouth*, the mouth is considered large. It suggests one who is likely to have many friends to talk to and who is generous with words. Family tends to be very important to those who have Full Lips and a *Wide Mouth*. Full Lips on a *Narrow Mouth* tell of one who strongly expresses to only a few. And, when Full Lips *stick out* this suggests an impulsive and, quite possibly, a self-indulgent individual.

On a first date with a Full Lips Individual you may find him or her to be very expressive. This is a positive sign, for when one with Full Lips keeps quiet this can reveal less interest in getting involved. However, Full Lips Individuals tend to love eating good food, and a less talkative Full Lips date may simply be expressing enjoyment in that particular sensual pleasure.

THIN LIPS

Thin Lips reveal those who hold back in verbal expression. When they do express feelings, they speak with sincerity.

Thin Lips Individuals have a gift for controlling the words they speak, a gift valuable in business where not everything is best revealed. When answering questions or giving directions, Thin Lips Individuals are apt to be clear and to the point. A *wise* Thin Lips Individual knows that it is often better to remain silent unless one has something constructive to say. Thin Lips Individuals are not forceful communicators like individuals with *thick* Full Lips.

Thin Lips suggest potential challenges when it comes to opening up to life's pleasures. Some with Thin Lips are picky eaters and some pick work as their focus over relationships. Thin Lips that are *tight* reveal a stubborn individual who might vocally lash out unexpectedly. When a Thin Lips person says "I love you" know that he or she truly means it.

Your Thin Lips partner may have difficulty expressing feelings. Words might come out in weird ways. Being non-judgmental can make communication easier, and a loving relationship can help. As communication grows, so may the lips. Lots of kissing might plump Thin Lips as well.

Opposites attract, but often it is the desire for a certain personality trait that is the attractor. One with Thin Lips may be attracted to a Full Lips Individual if it is his or her desire to get more enjoyment out of life and to express him- or herself more easily. And, a Full Lips Individual might be attracted to a Thin Lips Individual if it is his or her desire to have more control or refinement over what is revealed.

Often those with Thin Lips were criticized, not given sufficient acknowledgment, or held to high standards as children. As adults, they may be mistrustful of flattery or praise. Your partner with Thin Lips may not accept your compliments as easily as others might.

A Thin Lips Individual might send an indirect signal instead of saying how he or she feels. This is important to know when dating or in a relationship with a person with Thin Lips.

The two lips represent the two worlds

Of the two lips, the bottom is normally slightly bigger. The top lip is the feminine half, corresponding to the inner world and feelings. The bottom is the masculine half, corresponding to the outer world and doing. The Top Lip reveals *emotional expressiveness.*

FULLER TOP LIP

When the top lip is much bigger than the bottom, which is moderate in size, it is a Fuller Top Lip. A Fuller Top Lip reveals an emotionally expressive individual who likes excitement and might tend to exaggerate. Talk often turns to topics of a personal nature.

The gift of a Fuller Top Lip is the ease of expressing emotions. This can be beneficial in intimate relationships and can help actors in the work that they do. Animated attorneys with Fuller Top Lips can create drama and excitement in the courtroom.

Although most often tactful and diplomatic, challenges might arise in emotionally charged circumstances in which thinking through is the wise thing to do. Without care in these situations, Fuller Top Lip

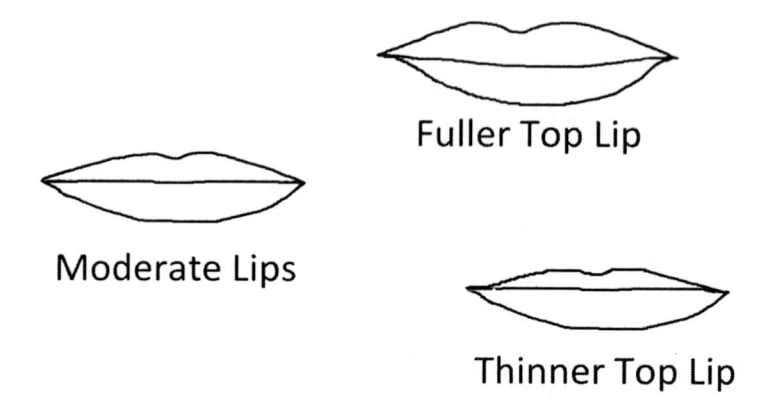

Fuller Top Lip

Moderate Lips

Thinner Top Lip

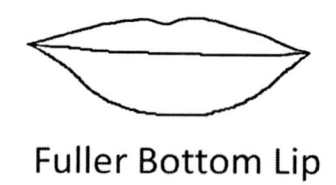

Fuller Bottom Lip

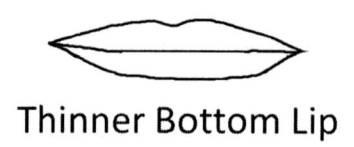

Thinner Bottom Lip

Individuals may unintentionally hurt others. There are challenges to speaking so freely.

If you have a Fuller Top Lip you may not hold back in expressing strong feelings. Make the words you say soft and sweet. You may have to eat them.

A Fuller Top Lip reveals a connection to inner feelings and intuition. This brings a gift when it comes to telling if another person's words are true. A Fuller Top Lip Individual is one you won't have an easy time lying to.

Your partner might wear a mustache over his Fuller Top Lip. This helps control the expressing of emotions but will not tone down his love of excitement.

THINNER TOP LIP

When the top lip is very thin and the bottom is of moderate size, it is a Thinner Top Lip. Thinner Top Lips tell of restraint in emotional expression. These individuals prefer keeping private matters private and are able to *outwardly* remain calm in situations in which others might become upset.

Thinner Top Lip Individuals take care in expressing emotions, and feelings expressed tend to be sincere. Because they hold back in verbal expression, Thinner Top Lip Individuals often have a strong desire for sex, which allows them to express and to feel. The top lip corresponds to feminine energy. Men tend to have Thinner Top Lips.

Bottoms are bigger

It is normal for the bottom lip to be bigger. The bottom lip moves more than the top. Bottom lips relate to the outer world and represent active expression of desires. The bottom lip reveals the *ability to persuade*.

FULLER BOTTOM LIP

When the bottom is noticeably big whereas the top lip appears moderate in size, it is a Fuller Bottom Lip. A Fuller Bottom Lip brings the gift of persuasion ability and reveals an individual who might indulge in sensual pleasures. Focus is on the outer world.

A Fuller Bottom Lip suggests appreciation of good food, good drink, and comfortable surroundings. Talk centers more on facts than feelings. This lip reveals a talent for talking readily, glibly, and convincingly.

Fuller Bottom Lip Individuals can convince others of their position and have an easier time getting people to believe what they say. A Fuller Bottom Lip suggests a competitive individual who may look for a good argument or debate. Politicians, salesmen, lawyers, and promoters of any type might benefit from having a Fuller Bottom Lip.

If someone with a Fuller Bottom Lip wants to see you again, but you are not sure you want to see him or her, the individual's persuasion ability might get you to agree.

A Fuller Bottom Lip partner is likely to have a gift for negotiating with salespeople. Your gift may be finding great bargains when shopping with him or her.

THINNER BOTTOM LIP

When the top lip looks moderate in size whereas the bottom lip appears to be much thinner, the lip is a Thinner Bottom Lip. A Thinner Bottom Lip reveals an individual who relates through feelings. This lip suggests a focus on the inner world.

When lips stick out, thoughts are spoken out

Not all individuals hold their lips the same way. Lips may stick out, be tightly pressed together, or may be loose. Lip "hold" suggests *force of verbal expression*.

THRUST OUT LIPS

When lips stick out strongly they are Thrust Out Lips. Sometimes these lips are held in the shape of a permanent "pout."

These individuals respond quickly. They may make good use of their gift working as public speakers, broadcasters, and salespeople. Impulsiveness is suggested, however. And, these individuals can be reactive. At times, they might regret what they say.

Thrust Out Lips that *aggressively stick out* suggest self-will, arrogance, and verbal aggression. They reveal a forceful communicator who will have the last word in a discussion or debate. These lips are a gift when fighting for a cause or a case. Thrust Out Lips Individuals whose lips aggressively stick out sometimes put pressure on themselves to prove their worth.

When the top lip thrusts out, the emphasis is on emotions. When the bottom thrusts out, the emphasis is on facts.

Some lips only *gently stick out*. These lips suggest a good-natured, sincere individual who enjoys talking. These lips don't reveal aggressive tendencies but tell of an impulsive individual with enthusiasm for life.

TIGHT LIPS

Lips that are held pressed together are Tight Lips. On some people, the top lip almost disappears. These individuals are not inclined to be very talkative; these lips tell of willpower and restraint. Tight Lip Individuals tend to be stubborn individuals who spend lots of time thinking.

When lips are *lightly* pressed together, thoughts are less serious, meditative, or contemplative. When lips are *tightly* pressed together it suggests thoughts are serious, heavy, or deep.

Tight Lips that disappear and form a *straight line* due to tightness are found on orderly, precise individuals. These lips show restraint in verbal expression. When it comes to romance, their head rules their heart. Serious scientists often have a straight line between Tight Lips. When a *curved line* is seen between Tight Lips, it suggests one who thinks creatively. Thoughtful individuals who spend much time in concentrated thought frequently have Tight Lips later in life.

Your date may be talking with lips that don't move. This suggests he or she is withholding information. Reading these lips gives you this information.

LOOSE LIPS

Lips held loosely are Loose Lips. Loose Lips Individuals live more in the external than the internal world. Ease of lip movement is the Loose Lips' gift. Performers, such as singers, often have looser lips, as do those who speak French well. The challenge for Loose Lips Individuals is in being too carefree in what they reveal; some are prone to careless talk.

When it comes to sensitive matters regarding work or personal information, you may want to limit what you tell a Loose Lips Individual. But if it is gossip you are seeking, go to him or her.

THE TEETH

Teeth tell of confidence, determination, decisiveness, and personal power. They reveal the ability to break down life experiences and learn from them. Teeth can give clues to sexual energy as well. Sparkling teeth suggests happiness, health, and fulfilled wishes. Problems with teeth suggest long standing uncertainty. Teeth correspond to the Water element.

When talking of teeth, size and shape matter

There is no way to measure teeth. Size and shape are determined subjectively. Teeth reveal *feelings of personal power and confidence in decision making.*

LARGE UPPER FRONT TEETH

The two center upper front teeth are naturally bigger than the others. When they are *very* large, they may be called Large Upper Front Teeth. They tell of confidence and a need to be noticed.

Large Upper Front Teeth reveal the gifts of personal strength, drive, and persistence. They suggest belief in self and in decisions made. These individuals hold on in the face of opposition. They also tend to be impatient.

Large Upper Front Teeth that are straight, strong, well-spaced, and healthy often reveal robust sexual energy. When these teeth are sharp, this suggests an individual who might be very assertive or sexually aggressive. And self-centered stubbornness is often a challenge for those with these big teeth.

If your date has Large Upper Front Teeth this suggests he or she desires constant recognition. If seeking to understand your partner more, recognize this desire as one of his or her natural needs.

SMALL UPPER FRONT TEETH

When the two center upper front teeth are not much bigger than the other teeth, they are Small Upper Front Teeth. They suggest an unassuming nature and one who does not typically brag or boast. Being assertive may be challenging for these individuals. They may not always receive the attention they deserve.

When *all teeth in a mouth are small* this can reveal an ambitious, active individual. This individual might try harder in order to succeed.

LARGE CANINE TEETH

The pointy teeth on the sides of the four upper front teeth are the canine teeth. They might be seen when one smiles. Canine teeth are made for tearing and ripping. When these teeth are much *longer* than the four teeth between them, they are Large Canine Teeth. Large Canine Teeth suggest some degree of aggression.

Large Canine Teeth reveal a powerful drive to succeed. When used wisely, this can bring success. Often those with these teeth are forceful in going after what they want. When Large Canine Teeth are *very large and sharp*, there is the potential to "destroy" weak individuals with harsh words or hurtful actions. Those with these teeth would be wise to be aware of this. Kindness has more power than force.

STRAIGHT TEETH

Teeth that are straight and even are Straight Teeth. They tell of a logical approach, inner strength, and balance. Straight Teeth Individuals tend to have an easier time making decisions and are confident about the decisions they make. They are less likely to go back and forth on decisions. Straight Teeth suggest one who learns quickly.

Straight Teeth that are strong, well-spaced, and healthy suggest a good amount of sexual energy. Straight Teeth suggest an optimistic individual who is prepared to take emotional risks.

Straight Teeth also often indicate an honest person. If one with Straight Teeth is *young*, however, this may or may not be true.

CROOKED TEETH

Teeth going in different directions are Crooked Teeth. They reveal individuals who see all sides of an issue and are open to different points of view. This is a gift to the individual and a blessing to others. But Crooked Teeth can tell of the potential challenge of being moody and confused.

Crooked Teeth Individuals have a tendency to go back and forth on decisions; they take time making them. When *bottom teeth* are crooked, this suggests that time is needed before taking action. Crooked *top teeth* suggest vacillation when it comes to emotional decision making. Crooked Teeth don't mean one is dishonest, but they might reveal a person who says different things to different people. Crooked Teeth might also reveal that the gums aren't what they once were. Crooked Teeth sometimes reveal a person is getting old.

If you have Crooked Teeth and have recently started dating someone, you may feel like moving forward one day, while on other days you feel like starting over with someone new. Here is something that might help you: If the *upper third* of your face is largest, write a pro and con list; if the *middle third* is largest, ask yourself if the individual shares the same values as you. If the *lower third* of your face is the largest, rely on your gift of intuition. Do something physical. When out of your head, you may find the answer comes to you. The first answer you receive is your intuitive voice. Go with that.

If your partner has Crooked Teeth think of him or her as a thoughtful decision maker.

FRONT GAP

When there is a space between the two upper front teeth, it is a Front Gap. A Front Gap suggests one who boldly takes intuitive risks. When it comes to taking chances, he or she takes a leap of faith. A Front Gap can also reveal a traumatic loss in childhood.

When gaps are found between most of an individual's teeth this suggests no clear sense of direction, poor health, or old age. An individual can't stop getting older (without dying or transitioning), but the first two things he or she might be able to change.

THE CHIN

The chin reveals will and strength. It gives clues to character and shows physical focus. The chin tells upon what basis decisions are made; it tells the speed of action one takes. A chin reveals how a person stands up to disapproval and how he or she deals with things when life becomes tough. Deep pain shows up as lines and markings on the chin but a cleft chin, or a dimple, shows a need to be noticed. The chin corresponds to the Water element.

A strong chin reveals a strong will

The size of a chin is subjective and is relative compared to the size of the face. When one has a long lower face he or she tends to have a Long Chin. Strong chins are large and firm. Chin size reveals *perseverance*.

LONG CHIN

A Long Chin reveals a physically based individual who has a great deal of endurance and perseverance. A long chin suggests a strong will. A strong will suggests a long life. Long Chin individuals often live a long time. The best part of their life may come later in life.

A *broad* Long Chin tells of the ability to recover quickly from adversity. A Long Chin and *full cheeks* suggests the gift of a powerful voice.

The longer the chin, the shorter the forehead will be. You may find your Long Chin partner does not spend much time in thought before taking action. Consider the chin's length when your partner wants to take back what he or she said.

SHORT CHIN

When a chin is short compared to the rest of the face, it is a Short Chin. A Short Chin reveals one who is mentally or emotionally based. A Short Chin Individual with a *large forehead* may have intellectual gifts. A Short Chin Individual with most *length in the middle face* might have a nose for money.

A Short Chin suggests a lesser amount of endurance. Short Chin Individuals most often do not desire to work long and hard into old age. These individuals are less likely to have a problem retiring early and enjoying life.

Men who wish to hide a Short or Small Chin may grow a beard. This can add the look of length, as well as the look of strength, but it won't add years to the time they wish to work.

SMALL CHIN

When a Short Chin is *narrow and delicate*, it is a Small Chin. It is similar to a Short Chin and contains many of the gifts. But, it tells of a gentler nature, lack of aggressive tendencies, and an individual likely to be hard on him- or herself. Those with this chin can be quite sensitive to criticism and benefit from encouragement and support.

Small Chin Individuals are not physical risk takers. To live a long life, Small Chin Individuals need to take care of their health. It may be up to them to nurture themselves. A lower level of competitiveness is suggested in this chin. And for them, this can be a gift.

BROAD CHIN

A Broad Chin is a powerful chin. It reveals a *strong* physical base, a very confident individual, and one who does not give up easily. It shows a sturdy nature and one who has an easier time staying grounded. Managers and directors of large corporations often have a Broad Chin.

Broad Chin Individuals are physically and emotionally tough. They have a sense of justice and fight for what they believe in; their feelings tend not to be hurt *easily*. Broad Chin Individuals are determined and persistent. Stubbornness and aggressiveness are their challenges.

A Broad Chin partner might have more trouble expressing emotional feelings than expressing physical ones.

LONG-BROAD CHIN

A Long-Broad Chin reveals traits found both in a Long Chin and a Broad Chin. It suggests tireless energy and an individual who is athletic or has the gift to be. This chin shows both power and willpower and one who is able to bounce back quickly from adversity.

These are strong individuals who tend to find pleasure in work and sex. If you are single and seeking, you may ask, "Where can I find one?"

Style of action is shown in the shape

The bottom of the chin comes in various shapes. The basic shapes are straight, square, round, and pointed.

If a beard is covering the shape of the chin, consider the beard the chin's bottom. Read the beard's shape if you can't see the chin. A beard's shape reveals how an individual desires to be seen. A chin's shape shows *style of action*.

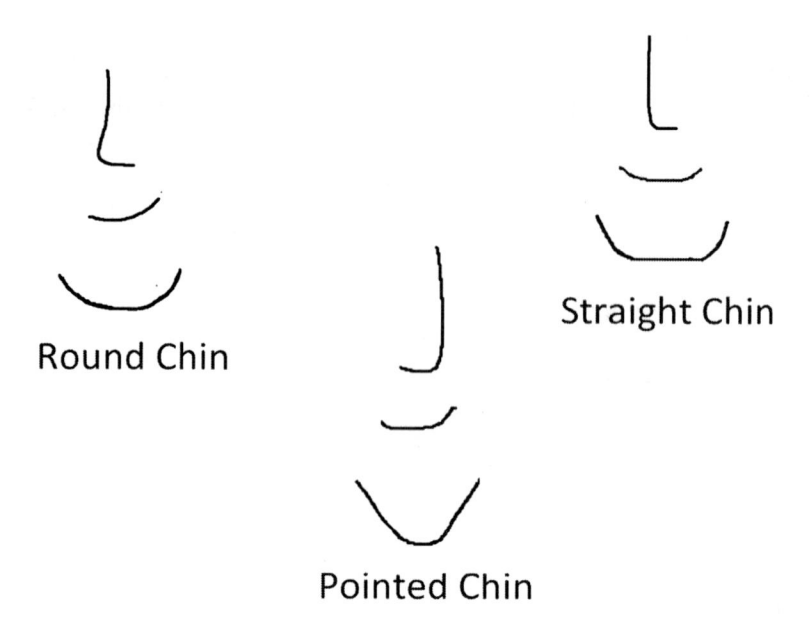

Round Chin

Straight Chin

Pointed Chin

STRAIGHT CHIN

When the chin's bottom is straight, it is a Straight Chin. A Straight Chin reveals a straightforward style of action, a focus on getting the job done, and gifts of logic and common sense. Motivated by their beliefs, Straight Chin Individuals make decisions based on principle. As disciplined individuals, they have the potential challenge of being rigid. They tend to like following carefully prepared plans.

A Straight Chin partner will typically take action in a methodical, orderly way. This may not always be your way of doing things.

SQUARE CHIN

When a chin is straight and wide, it is a Square Chin. A Square Chin is a blockier version of the Straight Chin and reveals many of the same attributes, as well as some additional ones. Their style of action is powerful.

Square Chin Individuals are strong characters who tend to be physically demonstrative. They have high energy, fight for what they believe, and often have a rough way of expressing themselves. Square

Chin Individuals don't like to compromise or negotiate, and some form enemies as a result. This chin tells of tenacity and endurance; these individuals don't give up.

A fighting spirit may be beneficial in youth, but in old age may keep others away. However, fighters who stick up for themselves in their senior years are unlikely to be taken advantage of. Square Chin Individuals may spend many years as seniors; this chin suggests a long life.

A Square Chin partner will not be happy in a subordinate position at work or in a relationship.

ROUND CHIN

When there is a curve to the chin's bottom, it is a Round Chin. Round Chin Individuals tend to have a pleasing nature, they like being around people, and most often have a strong sense of family. Their style of action suggests concern for others.

Round Chins reveal an unselfish, cooperative, and diplomatic style of action, which can bring success in social situations, in work, and in life. When making a decision, Round Chin Individuals tend to listen to all sides and consider others' opinions. A *very narrow* Round Chin reveals one who acts with tenderness but also indicates less grounding and less strength than a chin with more broadness to it.

A Round Chin partner gets what he or she wants through mutual agreement. Roundness suggests flexibility, adaptability, and a person willing to compromise.

A Round Chin date or mate is likely to have great care and concern for family and friends. This noble trait might mean less time with you as time will be needed for others.

POINTED CHIN

When a chin narrows to a point, it is a Pointed Chin. A Pointed Chin reveals a need to be in control. These individuals' style of action is motivated by self-interests; decisions made are often based on *their way.* It is important to Pointed Chin Individuals that they get their point across.

Pointed Chins suggests intelligent but moody individuals. Their swings in mood can cause difficulty making decisions. Their actions can be unpredictable. They are oftentimes oversensitive. Restlessness is in their nature; indeed, they need constant stimulation. However, they do tend to be charming, fun, friendly, and social.

A Pointed Chin Individual tends to have a strong sense of purpose. When one has a strong sense of purpose, there is often a stronger need to stay in control in order to stay focused and on track.

If requesting something of your Pointed Chin date, be sure to explain if the request is unclear. If it feels like an order, he or she is likely to resist.

Stubbornness can be seen from the side

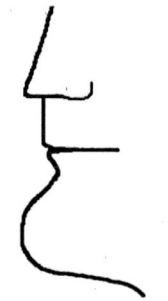

Some chins angle out. Some angle in. Look at the face from the side, that is, the profile view, to help determine this. Chin angle suggests *speed of action*.

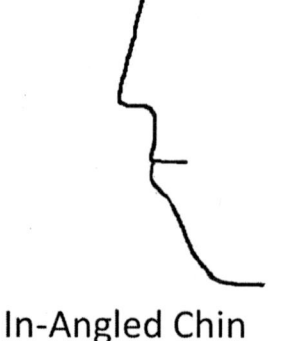

OUT-ANGLED CHIN

When the chin protrudes, it is an Out-Angled Chin. This chin reveals gifts of strong will, courage, and physical endurance. These individuals are *slow to take action* and are known for their stick-to-it-iveness. The greater the chin thrust, the more stubborn one will be. When an Out-Angled Chin juts out in the shape of a handle, this can tell of a desire to hoard wealth.

Out-Angled Chins reveal individuals who are determined, persistent, and confident in their beliefs. This chin suggests a fighting spirit and one not easily intimidated. These individuals desire to live life on their own terms, a gift that can sometimes bring challenges in work and love.

Out-Angled Chin Individuals are cautious; they won't be hurried into making decisions and may drag their feet when it comes to getting things done. When the chin tilts up, or looks "pushed in," this tells of extra strong resistance. This individual will move only if he or she wants to. When jaw muscles tighten, it reveals an individual unlikely to budge.

An Out-Angled Chin partner will want the last word in an argument.

If you are dating an Out-Angled Chin Individual who is interested in you, you have found one who won't give up easily. This can be important in making the relationship work. An In-Angled Chin Individual is more likely to retreat at the first sign of trouble. But, patience may be needed if you are looking for more than a dating relationship. When it comes to moving forward, an Out-Angled Individual is often slow moving and is likely to procrastinate.

IN-ANGLED CHIN

A chin that slants back from the mouth to any degree is an In-Angled or receding chin. The greater degree of the slant, the more the traits described below will apply.

An In-Angled Chin suggests one who *acts quickly*; oftentimes this is a gift. These individuals take care of business without wasting time. They like fast decisions and speedy results. They like fast service, fast conversation, and fast attention. Some may be restless, impatient, or impulsive. In-Angled Chin Individuals sometimes do not give enough thought to a matter and are inclined to act on a hunch.

This chin can reveal a lack of physical endurance and potential challenge of giving up too easily. These In-Angled Chin Individuals try to avoid conflict, which can make working with them easier. They are quicker to give in, let go of arguments, and prefer to resolve problems quickly. They are not fighters, but if they do fight it is most often for the rights of others. This chin can reveal an individual who has been dominated in the past.

Your In-Angled Chin partner may have a gift for learning quickly. Because it is not in their nature to be stubborn, In-Angled Chin Individuals tend not to willfully persist doing what is not working. They learn their lesson and make a change.

If you are meeting an In-Angled Chin Individual for the first time, be on time or early. If you are late, this individual might give up and leave before you arrive.

Full Double Chins

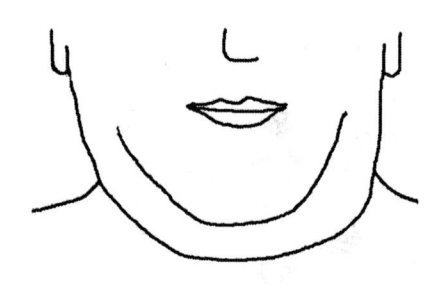

FULL DOUBLE CHIN

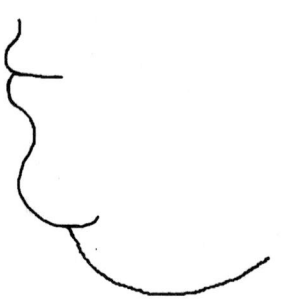

When an individual has a full chin and a second one, it is a Full Double Chin. A Full Double Chin shows a gift for enjoying life and an individual others tend to enjoy being around. A Full Double Chin can tell of a talent for making money and might reveal one who is generous with it.

A Full Double Chin suggests a passionate, sensual nature and a person who appreciates pleasures of the physical world. This chin reveals an earthy individual who is slow to take action but is not necessarily stubborn. There is much grounding seen in this chin.

When a person develops a Full Double Chin after age 60, this is said to bring a double dose of happiness in late life.

THE JAW

The jaw tells of stamina, determination, and power. Physical strength, emotional strength, strength of conviction, and how one handles conflicts are revealed in the jaw. The jaw corresponds to the Wood element.

Strength is seen in the width

To judge a jaw's width, look at the amount of bone below the ears. Jaw width is a *measure of strength*.

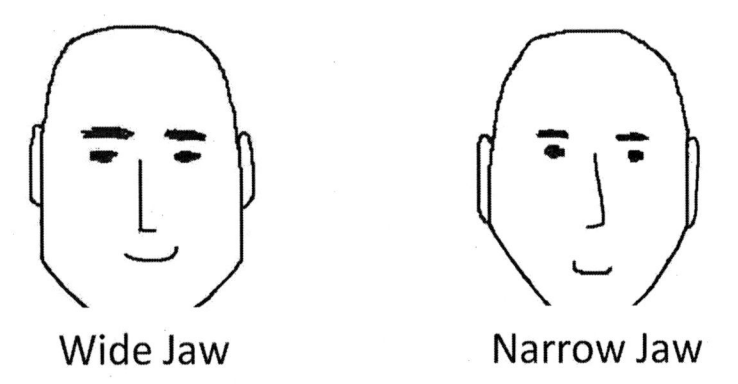

Wide Jaw   Narrow Jaw

WIDE JAW

A Wide Jaw looks strong and reveals abundant strength. It conveys determination and suggests one rooted in his or her beliefs. Wide Jaw Individuals go after what they want in life, which gives them the ability to achieve high status. Wide Jaws tells of a need to be noticed and most Wide Jaw Individuals are.

Wide Jaws suggest authority. Wide Jaw Individuals are fighters who don't give up once their mind is made up. Most people respect them for their principled beliefs. But some with a *very* Wide Jaw might alienate others by being aggressive or domineering, which they have the potential to be. The wider the face, the more confidence revealed.

Stamina and strength are seen in a Wide Jaw. Many of these individuals are physically gifted; some compete as athletes. When the jaw is defined and not flabby, this suggests strong sexual potential, another physical gift. Emotional strength is revealed as well. These are tough individuals who stay strong through difficult times. A Wide Jaw that is well defined suggests strength in old age.

Wide Jaw Individuals tend to be highly principled and most often can be counted on to keep their word. If in a relationship with a Wide Jaw Individual, you will be expected to keep your word as well. And, those with a Wide Jaw have expectations of getting what they want. They are tenacious. Expect a fight of sorts if you decide to move on.

A Wide Jaw date is likely to have a take charge attitude and be opinionated. If your partner has a Wide Jaw you already know this.

NARROW JAW

A Narrow Jaw angles in and reveals an individual who gives in more easily. A Narrow Jaw suggests a lesser amount of power and conviction. This can be a gift; the jaw's non-aggressive look allows others to approach a Narrow Jaw Individual more easily.

Narrow Jaw Individuals are not naturally fighters and, when possible, they avoid disputes and heated discussions. They are open to other's opinions, suggestions, and beliefs. They have an easier time than one with a Wide Jaw accepting that someone else might know more than they do when it comes to certain things. They tend to be easier to work with and people are more apt to offer them the support they might need. Possible challenges for Narrow Jaw Individuals are lack of passion, less confidence, and uncertainty of beliefs.

A Narrow Jaw suggests a gift for sensing conflict and one who will want to stop it before it escalates. If on a date with a Narrow Jaw Individual, and you are looking for a good debate, have it with someone else.

THE CHEEKS and CHEEKBONES

Both cheeks and cheekbones reveal power as perceived by others. The cheekbones and the upper portion of the cheeks correspond to the Metal element. The lower portion of the cheeks corresponds to Earth.

Noticeable bones get noticed

Cheekbones may be prominent or hidden. In Western cultures, prominent cheekbones tend to be admired and are viewed as powerful, but Chinese face readers feel that more power is found in full, rounded, chubby cheeks. Cheekbones reveal *perceived power*.

PROMINENT CHEEKBONES

When cheekbones are well developed and are the widest part of the face, they are Prominent Cheekbones. Prominent Cheekbones draw attention; attention these individuals tend to seek. The sight of Prominent Cheekbones can intimidate others. Prominent Cheekbones Individuals are *perceived to have power* and authority.

Prominent Cheekbones are found on successful entrepreneurs and business leaders, as well as high achievers in the military, government, and sports. Any position demanding authority might be suitable for one with Prominent Cheekbones. But, Prominent Cheekbones Individuals can be demanding, and this may present challenges in relationships.

Prominent Cheekbones

Hidden Cheekbones

Full Cheeks

Sunken Cheeks

Prominent Cheekbones Individuals tend to be spirited in words and actions; they naturally seek challenges and change. They like travel, adventure, and need their work and love life to be interesting. Strong-willed and persistent, they have stubborn tendencies.

Prominent Cheekbones that are *high* suggest pride and high ideals. These individuals are idealistic about love. Prominent Cheekbones can attract jealousy or criticism from others; as a result, some of these individuals have trouble making or keeping friends. *Boney, sharp* cheekbones suggest one who may be forceful at times. This can keep others away.

Thick cheekbones suggest a rougher nature with possible combative tendencies. *Delicate* cheekbones suggest a nature, which is refined and less aggressive. Prominent Cheekbones covered with a fleshy *soft padding* have *less perceived power* but have a gift for attracting assistance. These individuals can draw more friends and may have an easier life.

A partner with Prominent Cheekbones may stay in a relationship but will not stay in a rut.

The partner with the most Prominent Cheekbones will want to be the boss. This goes for both business partnerships and romantic relationships.

HIDDEN CHEEKBONES

When cheekbones are difficult to see or when they are "flat," they are Hidden Cheekbones. Hidden Cheekbones don't stand out, giving these individuals a non-threatening look. This benefits them in gaining cooperation at work and in social situations and brings easy access to help.

More agreeable than aggressive in nature, Hidden Cheekbones Individuals often are found to be polite and well mannered. They tend to prefer routine over change. They are *not perceived to have power*, but in many circumstances this can be a gift.

Hidden Cheekbones suggests an individual who is not a power seeker. If a Hidden Cheekbones Individual is a boss or manager, he or she will likely be easygoing and undemanding. Hidden Cheekbones Individuals tend not to like asserting their authority to control others. A police or military officer with Hidden Cheekbones may want to consider another line of work.

Your partner with Hidden Cheekbones might be overlooked by some but may be a remarkably talented individual. He or she may have wonderful qualities, for example, honesty or compassion, or your partner may be a very thoughtful person.

Life can be seen in the fullness

Cheeks can be full or hollow. Cheeks correspond to the lungs and tell of how deeply one takes in life energy. Cheeks give clues to power, as well as an individual's interaction with others. Cheek fullness reveals *vitality*.

FULL CHEEKS

Cheeks with lots of padding are Full Cheeks. Some may look "chubby." Full Cheeks indicate *vitality* and reveal power that is hidden. A Full Cheeks Individual can be fat or thin.

Full Cheeks Individuals have a people-centered approach and a gift for connecting with others. They are seen as friendly individuals. Extra padding on cheeks brings softness to the face, which conveys approachability and a look that people trust. Full Cheeks don't intimidate. People tend to come forward to support those with Full Cheeks.

People have an easier time cooperating with those whose cheeks are padded. They tend to be less critical of them. And, Full Cheeks Individuals tend to be less critical of others. Full Cheeks tell of the ability to express emotions easily and the power to be assertive when needed. Full Cheeks suggest a gift for enjoying the pleasures of life and an individual who might have an easier time living it.

Those with *firm* Full Cheeks plus *long chins* are often gifted with powerful voices beneficial for singing or speaking. Full Cheeks *protruding to the sides* often tell of a natural healer. When Full Cheeks are *high*, this suggests one who might excel as an entrepreneur, politician, or leader.

Because Full Cheek Individuals have the ability to get help from others easily, and tend to be open to accepting it, they are less likely to drain their own energy and become depleted. Along with power, there is wisdom revealed in these cheeks.

HOLLOW CHEEKS

Hollow Cheeks suggest *reduced vitality* and possibly weakness of spirit. A Hollow Cheeks Individual may not be having the easiest time with life. These individuals may feel something is missing.

Hollow Cheeks can suggest one who has difficulty finding peace, with inner unrest always present. Sometimes, inner unrest stimulates an individual to become a high achiever, contributing his or her special gift to the world. An easier life may not have sparked such action.

Some people have cheeks that are naturally hollow due to weak lungs and less ability to take in air, but for many Hollow Cheeks are temporary. Tension, stress, or fear can cause shallow breathing and scattering of vitality, and this can hollow the cheeks. Depression and under eating may cause cheek depletion as well. When the temporary condition lifts, the cheeks fill out again.

If you have Hollow Cheeks and scattered vitality, you may find it helpful to unify your breathing with your own being through meditation. This can re-gather lost energy and encourage physical, mental, and emotional health. It can help you deal with stress.

If your partner has Hollow Cheeks, before making the above suggestion, be sensitive to him or her. Your Hollow Cheeks partner might be under extreme pressure and might view any suggestions as additional pressure. If this is the case, he or she might benefit more from understanding, compassion, and love.

Section III

ANOTHER LOOK:

The Face and the Five Chinese Elements

THE FACE AND THE FIVE CHINESE ELEMENTS

The Five Element Theory originated in ancient China and is used in Chinese Medicine, Face Reading, and Feng Shui.

Ancient Chinese philosophers and scientists were keen observers of nature. Observing nature they saw that all in the physical world was in a continual process of transformation. They came up with a theory to explain this occurrence. They distinguished five basic elements, each representing a dynamic quality of nature. Each element had a corresponding energy.

Ancient Chinese physicians found they could use the Five Element Theory in diagnosing and treating patients. They found it could also be used to read faces to ascertain a person's personality.

There are five basic elemental types named after each of the Five Elements. The Five Elements are: Wood, Fire, Earth, Metal, and Water. Depending on elemental type, an individual expresses him- or herself in a certain way. Each elemental type also has certain gifts and challenges.

People consist of a combination of all elements, but the face shape and strongest facial features suggest the dominant element. The shape of the body, and the way a body moves, also gives clues to the dominant element.

Each element has corresponding physical aspects, but one need not have all the physical aspects to be a certain elemental type. However, the more characteristics an individual has that correspond to a particular element, the more obvious that element will be. Pure elemental types are rare, with Fire being the rarest.

Commonly, aging brings wisdom and a relaxing into mellowness of personality. When it comes to the energy corresponding to each element, the energy of a person in his or her senior years might change a bit. A Fire person is apt to be less animated and excitable as he or she grows old and a Wood Individual may still have a strong drive but be less driven or competitive than in his or her youth.

When doing a Five Element reading:

1) Look at the face shape. Each of the Five Elements has a corresponding face shape.

2) Look at the most noticeable features and body shape. Learn the element to which they relate.

When it is difficult to determine the dominant element, this could mean there is a blending of all elements or it might reveal two dominant elements. It is very common for people have two or three elements show up strongly.

Modern lifestyles can impact face or body shape and sometimes this makes it more difficult to determine the elemental type. A Wood face and body is naturally slender and a Water face and body is naturally curvy or somewhat plump. If a Wood Individual overeats, he or she will become fat. If a Water Individual diets, he or she may become thin. Although over- or under-eating can alter the appearance of the container, the features contained are less likely to change.

WOOD

WOOD FACE SHAPE: Inverted Triangle or Rectangular

WOOD FEATURES: Eyebrows, brow bone, jaw, temples

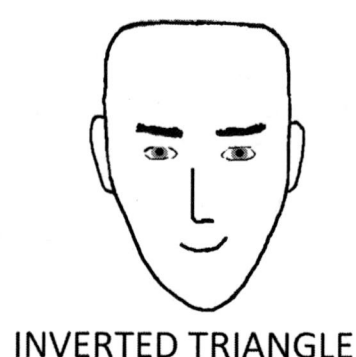

INVERTED TRIANGLE WOOD FACE   **RECTANGULAR WOOD FACE**

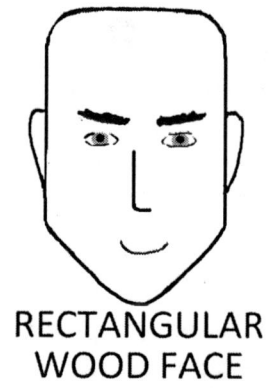

Wood suggests growth and expansion. When envisioning Wood energy, think of a tree. A Wood face has a tall forehead and narrow cheeks. When much wider at the top a Wood face is an Inverted Triangle shape, but when the jaw is very strong, a Wood face takes on more of a rectangular shape. Wood faces are long and thin.

When it comes to physique, Wood bodies are wiry with lean, sinewy muscles. Most often, a Wood Individual is tall. When Wood energy manifests in a short physique, Wood energy will have a more outward than upward movement. Think of this type of Wood as a bush as opposed to a tree.

Features that correspond to Wood are the eyebrows, brow bone, jaw, and temples. Wood energy shows in eyebrows that are strong, thick, higher at the outer ends, and long. Wood is revealed in an observable ridge above the eyebrows; this is a showing of the brow bone and tells of drive and determination. A well-defined jaw corresponds to Wood energy. The wider the jaw, the more rooted in beliefs an individual will be. And, indented temples show Wood energy.

Certain aspects of other features also give clues to Wood energy. For example, Wood is indicated in ears that are broadest at the top and high-set. When ears and chin stick out this reveals Wood.

Thick, short hair that sticks up suggests rising wood energy. Many Wood Individuals wear their hair in an easy-to-care for sporty style; they have more on their mind to think about. Wood eyes tend to be intense and often sit higher in the socket but Wood eyes might also have a kindly look as Wood corresponds to compassion and benevolence.

Each element symbolizes a flow of energy. Wood energy moves up and out slowly. Wood needs to grow and expand. Wood needs challenges to move energy that might otherwise become stuck. When a Wood Individual's energy is stuck, his or her upper body will look tense or rigid.

Wood Individuals are the most intellectual of the elemental types. When ideas come, they expand on them. They have a gift for transforming thoughts into things. When they stop evolving, they easily become depressed. They have a high level of tenacity, drive, and competitiveness. Wood is about "doing." It is important for them to use their gifts. But, they do need balance so that they do not burn out. However, taking time out might be a challenge for some of these individuals.

Expanding their mind is more important than expanding their wallet

Wood Individuals tend not to be focused on wealth and don't take a job for the money. Aspiring to high ideals is where their fortune lies. They are rooted in their beliefs; they inspire others and initiate change. They seek a meaningful and purposeful life.

Wood Individuals tend to be socially conscious and altruistic. When very stressed, however, Wood Individuals can become angry easily or fly into a rage. They are naturally intense.

Wood Individuals are born leaders who are dedicated and persevere. They may find success as corporate leaders or politicians. They can excel in careers in the arts, sciences, education, or research; they may find success as consultants, strategists, and urban planners. Wood Individuals make great trial attorneys due to their intellectual mind and love for argument and debate. The strength of Wood energy is in the ability to be active. Many are gifted athletes.

When it comes to their home, they often are drawn to wood walls, wood floors, and wood furniture, as well as plants and plenty of books. Wood homes have a common-sense, organized look. To them, acquiring mastery in another language may be more important than having more stuff. They need to move forward and feel depressed when feeling stuck. Due to a desire to grow and expand as time goes on a Wood person might want a larger living space.

When it comes to clothes, Wood goes for practicality. They like easy-to-care-for classic or sporty styles that don't restrict their movement. When it comes to climate, they don't want too much air moving. Wood Individuals are adverse to wind.

It may be best not to ask your Wood partner for advice about an important matter unless you intend to follow his or her advice. Disregarding your Wood partner's advice might not be taken lightly and you may end up with two problems and not just your original one.

Wood Individuals think in advance. Making plans is important to a Wood Individual because it represents movement. Ask your Wood partner, "What's the plan?" and he or she most likely will have one. In an emergency or disaster situation, count on your Wood partner to be prepared.

Your Wood date or partner will likely find it easier to relax when watching television if he or she feels he or she is learning something.

FIRE

FIRE FACE SHAPE: Tapered forehead, broad jaw.

FIRE FEATURES: Points on corners and tips of features. Sparkling bright eyes, freckles, dimples, and lines.

FIRE FACE

Fire energy embodies liveliness and excitement. Fire energy rises rapidly. To think of a Fire face, think of a flame. A Fire face has prominent cheekbones and a broad jaw. The forehead appears "tight" and narrows to a "cone" shape.

Features that correspond to Fire are known as "points" and "tips." A Fire face is bonier than most and has points at the tips of the nose, ears, and lips. Brows are arched; they point up in the middle. Jaw, nose, and cheekbones are defined. Hair might be worn sticking up in a spiky style.

Fire skin has a slight red undertone and due to a Fire person's expressive nature, lots of lines. Freckles indicate Fire energy. Eyes are a Fire feature. Fire eyes sparkle. Dimples reveal extra magnetism and charm. When an indentation is found at the tip of a nose, this suggests one whose work is seeking purpose. It is important that Fire Individuals love what they do!

Red hair belongs to Fire and, if not completely red, most Fire Individuals' hair has at least some red highlights. Early balding is also a Fire trait. It suggests that heat in the brain is burning the hair off the head.

Fire gets noticed and Fire Individuals want to be

The Fire physique is small and sturdily built, with narrow hips and a straight back. The posture may be described as "alert." When fit and toned as they often are, Fire Individuals love displaying their body in dance, sports, or some physical way. They are rarely fat. They have dynamic, captivating personalities along with a commanding presence. Often, they are more interested in attention than in money.

Those with a lot of Fire characteristics are considered "fiery." The more an individual physically corresponds to the Fire element, the more the corresponding personality traits apply. Most Fire Individuals do not have a Fire face shape *and all* the Fire features. A pure Fire Individual is *rare* and would be very intense. Fire often combines with Wood; when this is the case, the cheekbones are the widest part of the face.

It is difficult for a Fire person to keep still. They talk fast, always have things to talk about, change the subject of a conversation rapidly, and talk a lot with their hands. Their gestures are quick. Their expressive eyes communicate a great deal. They love sharing their ideas and dreams.

When it comes to work, Fire Individuals are natural for careers in entertainment, media, the arts, and public relations. They are great at influencing and inspiring people. With their enthusiasm, they make good motivational speakers. And a Fire Individual's pointed features, especially the nose tip, reveals a gift for investigating matters. They can excel in careers calling for them to "look into" things and may find success in undercover work. This type work is different from day to day, gives them room to move, can be risky, and might provide the excitement they crave.

Fire Individuals love fun and adventure; they are stimulating to be around. When things get boring, they create drama to stir things up. They tend to be impulsive with a short attention span. Fire's energy rises rapidly. They are not rude, but they do have difficulty holding back. When they are excited, they might interrupt when others are speaking. In spite of this, manners are very important to them.

Fire corresponds to the emotion of joy, but when stressed or extremely vulnerable, they can become anxious, scattered, or sad. They want to be kind but at times can be fierce or vicious. When affected emotionally, physically, or spiritually, they are prone to ailments of the heart.

Fire Individuals' feelings are read easily and change easily. They love being in love and have a deep-seated longing for passionate love. Fire ears are pointed at the top and broadest in the middle, indicating both comfort and impulsiveness in taking emotional risks. Fire ears tend to stick out more than most. It is important that Fire Individuals stay connected to others, but they need to be sensitive to others' boundaries. The heart corresponds to Fire and is responsible for emotions. All lines on a face are Fire lines.

A Fire Individual requires frequent validation; that is just who the individual is. A strong desire for love, however, can be a major challenge, making life a series of emotional ups and downs. Learning to see love everywhere, and to find love within, may be a Fire Individual's life lesson. It would be wise for a Fire Individual to seek self-love first

Fire likes what looks hot but is adverse to heat

When it comes to Fire Individuals' homes, the "feeling" of the home is important. They like bold colors and dramatic shapes. Inside their home, they don't rest in one spot but move from place to place. If their home is small, they might walk in and out or up and down the alley or street. They tend to be a bit claustrophobic; they don't like clutter. The bigger their home, the more things they can keep. They love candles burning, but when it comes to climate, they are affected by heat.

When it comes to clothes, Fire Individuals are drawn to what is fun, bold, and edgy, such as bright colors, unusual cuts, and geometric patterns. Fire women like what is sexy. They go for spiked heels and lingerie more erotic than functional. When they wear sandals they may paint their toes with glitter or red. An attention-grabbing hat might be on a Fire Individual's head.

Fire Individuals walk briskly. If you notice your Fire partner plodding along, pay attention. Something is likely wrong.

Clefts on chins are found on playful and adventurous people who desire to be admired. Clefts on chins are often seen on Fire Individuals.

When things get difficult in a relationship, rather than work on the relationship, a Fire Individual might instead just move on. Fire Individuals can be reactive, unpredictable, and changeable. What stays constant is their need for love.

When talking to your Fire partner, you may have an easier time holding his or her attention if you hold his or her hand or have your arms around him or her.

EARTH

EARTH FACE SHAPE: Can be Square or Round

EARTH FEATURES: Large features in general. The mouth, lips, upper eyelids, and lower cheeks correspond to the Earth element.

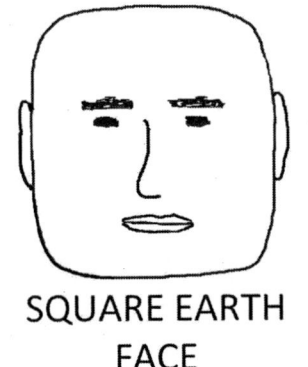

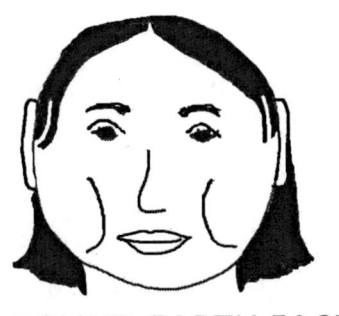

SQUARE EARTH FACE

ROUND EARTH FACE

Earth suggests stability. To think of Earth, think of things solid such as mountains, rocks, and ground. Earth energy manifests in two face shapes, square and round. An Earth Face is short in length.

When *square*, this suggests one more business oriented. Earth Individuals with *square* faces have what it takes to work hard, make lots of money, and lead companies. They are durable; their actions are measured and deliberate; they are immovable when pursuing goals. A body of *square* Earth face is stocky, blockish, and sturdily built. Earth men with *square* faces tend to have large muscles.

When the Earth Face is *round* it reveals a nurturing nature and one who is focused on family. When it comes to work, they prefer working for others, as connection is very important to them. They are happiest when caring for others but need to be careful they do not smother others. The Earth physique of a person with a *round* face may be described as rounded, plump, or fleshy.

Features that correspond to Earth are the mouth, lips, upper eyelids, and lower cheeks. A large mouth with full lips suggests Earth energy and love of sensual pleasures such as good food, good drink, and comfortable surroundings. Earth Individuals make excellent hosts, like socializing, and tend to have a wide circle of friends. But when vertical lines are found above a mouth, this reveals one who overextends him- or herself and needs to learn to ask for what he or she needs.

Plump lower cheeks correspond to Earth and may be known as "moneybags." They show a gift for accumulating energy and money. Lower cheeks that are flat and sag indicate support, energy, or money may be lost; these cheeks appear depleted.

Although the nose corresponds to the Metal element, a *broad* nose shows Earth energy. A *broad bridge* suggests ease in handling multiple streams of income and a *broad base* suggests support is given easily and easily received. Support can be emotional or financial.

Earth Individuals are grounded. They walk without lifting their feet very high off the floor. They give considerable thought before making a move and take carefully calculated risks. Logical and practical, they tend to be conformists, preferring things done in a traditional way. Procrastination may be a problem at times for Earth people.

Earth Individuals tend to be supportive and have a talent for comforting others. They are trustworthy in nature and make good confidants. Although normally calm and strong emotionally, when stressed, an Earth Individual tends to worry or obsess. When it comes to dress, they like comfortable clothes. At night they are likely to settle down in flannel pajamas or an old-tee shirt on a sturdy, comfy bed.

Earth is stable, but might fall into a rut

Earth is a fixed element, so a permanent home is important. Because of their durable nature they want a home that is solidly built. They desire comfort; their homes tend to be cozy and inviting. Earth energy represents nourishment, so the kitchen is often an Earth Individual's favorite part of the house. Outside, an Earth Individual may enjoy doing earthy things such as watering the garden, but when it comes to climate, Earth is adverse to damp.

If looking for someone who values stability in a relationship, consider an Earth Individual. If you have trouble sticking to someone, at least you'll have someone who tends to stick. However, if you are also an Earth elemental type, be aware that *two* Earth Individuals together can become *too* comfortable. Care needs to be taken to avoid allowing an Earth relationship to stagnate or fall into a rut.

If in a relationship with an Earth Individual, friends and/or family are likely to play a big part in your partner's life.

METAL

METAL FACE SHAPE: Oval or Oblong.

METAL FEATURES: Nose, upper cheeks, cheekbones, space between features.

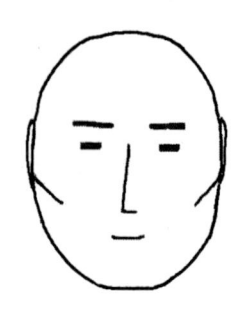

METAL FACE

Metal is contained, controlled, and refined. To think of Metal, think of a coin, for there are two sides to these individuals. Outside they might appear cold or aloof but inside they tend to be very sensitive. To the world, Metal Individuals might seem proper and put together. Perfection is important to them.

A Metal face is oval and widely set. It conveys balance. When one has a Metal face, the upper, middle, and lower regions are equal in length, and there is a good amount of *space* between each feature.

Features that correspond to Metal are the nose, upper cheeks, and cheekbones. Metal Individuals have high cheeks, high eyebrows, sharp cheekbones, and a straight nose. The chin and forehead are typically broad; hair is neat, orderly, and tends to be straight. Metal eyes are small and at times seem to be looking within. When it comes to flow of energy, Metal energy is drawn in. A Metal mouth is narrow and Metal lips are thin. Ears tend to lie flat to the head.

When it comes to physique, Metal might not look strong, their bones tend to be delicate, their body often slim. Metal Individuals move slowly and deliberately. When they walk, they walk lightly; you may not hear them coming. When they talk their speech might be clipped.

When it comes to career, Metal's attention to detail is an asset in legal or technical positions, and they can find success in the design field. They like organizing things and do well where they can put this talent to use. Metal Individuals are predisposed toward justice and strive to do what is right. Being balanced and logical, they make good leaders.

Metal suggests decisiveness and an individual who acts on decisions. They prefer rules, regulations, and procedures and when following them make decisions quickly. Once a decision has been made, a Metal Individual tends not to go back on it. Once they end a friendship it is over.

Metal itself is hard and Metal Individuals are hard on themselves

Being perfectionists, Metal Individuals often prefer to take matters into their own hands. When they do things their own way, they have a better chance of having things come out the way they like. Metal Individuals are ethical, go by the book, and may not tolerate those who frequently bend rules. They tend to be fair in dealing with others but are not known to be the easiest people to live with. Melancholy and grief are associated with the Metal element and therefore are possible challenges. They can have trouble letting go; they get stuck in nostalgia. Disciplined and controlled individuals, when stressed they lack self-esteem.

Metal Individuals tend to be self-contained and can be content in a compact living space provided there is room to organize and store belongings. Their home is likely to be filled with metal-based furniture, an assortment of gadgets, and the latest electronics. They like occupying themselves by fixing things. Due to their sensitive nervous system, décor in pastels or monochromatic colors is best. If a Metal Individual's home is cluttered with too many things, this shows difficulty in releasing and draws in a Metal person's already inward flowing energy further.

When it comes to clothes, Metal chooses outfits that are structured, well made, and made with attention to detail. They have a refined taste and are drawn to quality. Inwardly focused, colors worn tend to be subdued. They are not flashy attention seekers.

When it comes to climate, Metal suggests one not fond of dryness. The topic of climate usually does not come up on a first date, but if looking for a serious, long-term relationship, you may want to give thought to what climate suits you. Then, ask your potential mate what he or she prefers.

Your Metal partner might want things a certain way, which won't always make sense to you. Metal often has to have things a certain way in order to stay calm and balanced. One can never really know what is going on inside another individual.

Metal Individuals are known to have high standards and love boundaries. If you are a close friend of a Metal person, you have passed the test.

WATER

WATER FACE SHAPE: Irregularly round

WATER FEATURES: Ears, hairline, forehead, under-eye area, chin

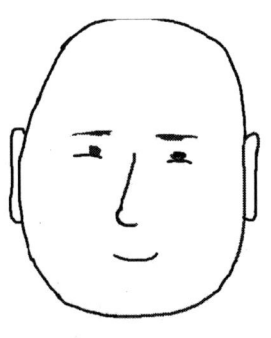

WATER FACE

To think of a Water face, think of a flowing stream or ocean. A Water face has no particular fixed shape, but tends to be roundish. It might look formless or unstructured; it often appears chubby and soft. You won't see bones in a Water face. These individuals need to have some things hidden.

Features that correspond to Water are the ears, hairline, forehead, under-eye area, and chin. When Water's energy flows freely, the skin under the eyes is clear; when their energy stagnates, dark rings appear. The eyes themselves tend to be smaller than average and often have a dreamy quality. They may seem to disappear into the skin when a Water Individual smiles. Mysterious and deep are words that describe a Water Individual.

When the Water element shows up strongly ears will be large with hanging lobes; the jaw will be undefined. Water features have curves; Water hair is wavy and thick. The eyebrows on a Water Individual may be broken or difficult to see; this reveals thinking is not done rigidly. Brows that are light colored reveal adaptability as well as a chameleon personality. The more prominent the individual's Water features, the more "watery" that individual will be.

A Water body has big bones and wide hips. It has a long spine, which helps Water Individuals bend and twist. Ankles and wrists are thick.

Water might lounge in the tub but may swim in money

Water is fluid and changes form easily, making Water Individuals flexible and adaptable. They can easily fit in with others and tend to be patient listeners. They are able to express thoughts and feelings clearly; they have strength in communication and they make good negotiators. They have a talent for bringing disparate people and ideas together and making sense of things.

There is much beneath the surface of a Water Individual. Their wisdom and intuition gives them the ability to sense opportunity and act on it. They have a gift for wealth, especially when it comes to making money in creative ways.

The Water element corresponds to courage; these individuals are quite comfortable taking risks. One of their strengths is in dealing with money. They can find success as bankers, financiers, or professional gamblers; they excel as entrepreneurs. Although most often courageous, fear arises when a Water Individual feels stressed.

Water Individuals do well in careers in which their work is different from day to day. They are drawn to out-of-the-ordinary jobs and occupations that involve travel. They love traveling for pleasure as well. They have a talent for taking innovative approaches; their resourcefulness brings opportunity in many fields. Water Individuals easily adapt to the challenges and changes that arise in life. Although outgoing, most often they are also private people. They don't like routine, but to get things done, scheduling is important.

Water symbolizes the subconscious and the emotional state of the mind. Water Individuals are often gifted when it comes to psychic ability. Water

Individuals make good therapists because of their deep understanding of feelings. The stronger the Water element, the smaller the eyes will be. This facilitates deep thinking, helps a Water Individual from becoming moody, and creates a sense of mystery.

To keep the mystery going, Water Individuals may cover up in sunglasses, sweatshirts, coats, boots, and hats. Water women are especially fond of sensual fabrics and flowing clothing.

Water indicates fluid movement and a dislike of restriction. When it comes to home, Water Individuals prefer large, open spaces, both inside and out. They like to live near water, such as a river, ocean, or lake. For many Water Individuals, a favorite place might be the bathtub. To accommodate their desire not to expose everything, Water Individuals need a few dark corners in their home. And, concerning climate, Water Individuals dislike cold.

Water needs a sense of freedom in relationships. When stressed, Water Individuals are not their usual adaptable selves and can be overly cautious, extra sensitive, or reactive. When unsure of themselves, they ask lots of questions. And when they are asked a lot of questions that they feel pressured to answer, they may avoid them, shut down, and pull away. They hate feeling confined.

You may find that a Water Individual knows more than what you told him or her. Water Individuals are known to have strong psychic abilities.

Because of their secretive nature, you may hurt your Water partner and not know it. A Water Individual reacts by retreating when he or she is hurt.

If meeting for a date, know that a Water Individual tends to be late.

LOVE IS AN ACTIVITY OF CONSCIOUSNESS

A new world is emerging; an energetic shift has taken place. The veil of separation is thinning and people are becoming increasingly aware of all living things, their effect on the earth, and their effect on each other. This new era births a movement from the love of power to the power of love.

As you awaken to the Divine qualities in others, you will find more loving people in your life, as well as more beauty, peace, and harmony in your world. Your vibration will rise, your light will increase, and this will impact the entire planet. Be understanding, compassionate, and tolerant toward all. *BE the love* you desire to receive. See all people evolving in goodness; even if this is not everyone's experience, in your world it will be. Love is an activity of consciousness. Be aware of your connection to everyone and everything.

BIBLIOGRAPHY

Brown, Simon. *Face Reading – Secrets of the Chinese Masters*. New York, NY: Sterling Publishing Co, Inc., 2007.

Bridges, Lillian. *Face Reading in Chinese Medicine*. St. Louis, Mo; Churchill Livingston, 2004.

Fuller, Mac, J.D.. *Amazing Face Reading*, U.S.: Mac Fuller, 1994

Haner, Jean. *The Wisdom of Your Face*. Carlsbad, CA: Hay House, Inc., 2008.

Kanto, Eric and Ilona. *Your Face Tells All*. Simi Valley, CA., Atophill Publishing,

Kuei, Chi An. *Face Reading*. New York, NY: M. Evans and Company, Inc., 1998.

Kushi, Michio. *Your Face Never Lies*. United Kingdom: Red Moon Press, 1976.

Machiocia, Giovanni. *The Foundations of Chinese Medicine*. Edinburgh: Churchill Livingstone, 1989.

McCarthy, Patrician. *The Face Reader*. New York, NY: Penguin Books, 2007.

Mitchell, M.D. *How to Read the Language of the Face*. New York, NY: The MacMillian Company, 1968.

Perdew, Harry, Ph.D. *It's More Than Words- Reading People from the Outside In*. Bloomington, IN: Authorhouse, 2006.

Rosetree, Laura. *I Can Read Your Face*. Silver Spring, MD: AHA! Experiences, 1988.

Rosetree, Rose. *The Power of Face Reading*. Sterling, VA: Women's intuitionWorldwide, 2001.

Rosetree, Rose. *Read People Deeper*, Sterling, VA: Women's Intuition Worldwide, 2008.

Stanton, M.O.,*The Enclycopedia of Face and Form Reading*, Philadelphia, PA: F.A.Davis Company, (Seventh Edition) 1922.

Tickle, Naomi R. *You Can Read a Face Like a Book*, United States: Daniels Publishing, 2003.

Shen, Peter. *Face Fortunes- The Ancient Chinese Art of Feature Reading*. Selangor Darul Ehsan, Malaysia: Pelanduk Publications, 1991.

Yap, Joey. *Mian Xiang, Discover Face Reading*. Kuala Lumpur, Malaysia: JY Books, 2005

Young, Lailan. *Secrets of the Face*. Boston, MA: Little Brown and Company, 1984.

Contact Information and Services

FACE READINGS

For a face reading by Debra Jeane Houle please visit www.FaceFortunes.com.

Others, such as attorneys, H.R. specialists, and casting directors may also be interested in her consultation services.

Email: DebraJeaneHoule@FaceFortunes.com .

BOOK

For additional copies or to purchase book in a different format:

www.TheFaceReadingForLoveBook.com

CLASSES, SEMINARS, and WORKSHOPS

www.FaceReadingForLove.com

CPSIA information can be obtained at www.ICGtesting.com
Printed in the USA
LVOW10s1657180514

386085LV00006B/51/P